JULIUS CAESAR

LEADERSHIP ▪ STRATEGY ▪ CONFLICT

NIC FIELDS

First published in Great Britain in 2010 by Osprey Publishing,
Midland House, West Way, Botley, Oxford OX2 0PH, UK
44-02 23rd St, Suite 219, Long Island City, NY 11101, USA

E-mail: info@ospreypublishing.com

© 2010 Osprey Publishing Ltd

A CIP catalogue record for this book is available from the British Library.

ISBN: 978 1 84603 928 7
E-book ISBN: 978 1 84603 929 4

Editorial by Ilios Publishing Ltd, Oxford, UK (www.iliospublishing.com)
Page layout by Myriam Bell Design, France
Index by David Worthington
Typeset in Stone Serif and Officina Sans
Maps by Mapping Specialists Ltd
Originated by PPS Grasmere, Leeds, UK
Printed in China through Worldprint Ltd

10 11 12 13 14   10 9 8 7 6 5 4 3 2 1

Artist's note

Readers may care to note that the original paintings from which the
colour plates in this book were prepared are available for private sale.
The Publishers retain all reproduction copyright whatsoever. All
enquiries should be addressed to:

Peter Dennis, Fieldhead, The Park, Mansfield, Notts, NG18 2AT, UK

The Publishers regret that they can enter into no correspondence upon
this matter.

Abbreviations

BC	Caesar *Bellum civile*
BG	Caesar *Bellum Gallicum*
DI	Suetonius *Divus Iulius*
Ad Att.	Cicero *Epistulae ad Atticum*
Ad fam.	Cicero *Epistulae ad familiares*

The Woodland Trust
Osprey Publishing are supporting the Woodland Trust, the UK's leading
woodland conservation charity, by funding the dedication of trees.

FOR A CATALOGUE OF ALL BOOKS PUBLISHED BY OSPREY
MILITARY AND AVIATION PLEASE CONTACT:

Osprey Direct, c/o Random House Distribution Center,
400 Hahn Road, Westminster, MD 21157
Email: uscustomerservice@ospreypublishing.com

Osprey Direct, The Book Service Ltd, Distribution Centre,
Colchester Road, Frating Green, Colchester, Essex, CO7 7DW
E-mail: customerservice@ospreypublishing.com

www.ospreypublishing.com

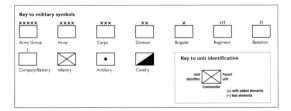

CONTENTS

INTRODUCTION

The fate of most of us is to vanish without trace in the mantle of history, and usually individuals who figure in history do so because another individual chooses to recount their deeds for posterity. Homer immortalized Achilles, as did Virgil for Aeneas; Plato, along with the unpretentious Xenophon, preserved the memory of Socrates. Caius Iulius Caesar, known to us as Julius Caesar and by common consent one of history's great men, naturally took care of his own reputation.

For us moderns the conquest of Gaul stands as the greatest of Caesar's achievements, yet at the time it was little other than a stepping stone in his struggle for power. In this Caesar had the great advantage of being a man of letters as well as a man of war, the embodiment of Mars and Minerva. It was a talent that enabled him to be, as the Romans said, his own herald. He wrote seven what he called 'Commentaries', *commentarii*, on his campaigns in Gaul, with a further three dealing with the subsequent war against his

former ally and political rival, Cnaeus Pompeius Magnus, better known as Pompey the Great. Additional *commentarii*, what we call books, were not written by Caesar himself but produced after his death by officers who had served under him, cover the final operations in Gaul and the remainder of the civil war.

By calling them *commentarii* the author meant they were not drab history but more like a commander's front-line dispatches enlivened by letters exchanged between Caesar and the Senate. In all probability he wrote all seven *commentarii* on the Gallic War, the *Bellum Gallicum*, in the winter of 52–51 BC (a view not universally accepted), meaning of course they were published at a particularly opportune time. Others may have mocked Caesar for his balding pate and his sexual adventures, but the image of him revealed by the *commentarii* – soldier, statesman and strategist – surely did much to shush the snapping swarm and ensure the popularity he needed to win in the eventual showdown with Pompey as they presented a Roman Caesar who was more than the equal of Pompey the great conqueror of the east.

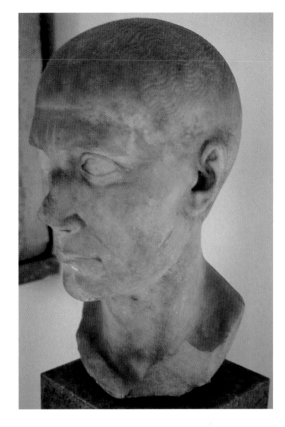

Marble bust of Caesar (Palermo, Museo Archeologico Regionale, N.I. 1967), a Iulio-Claudian copy of a 1st-century original, provenance unknown. Of all the figures of antiquity, his spectacular demise on the Ides of March would make him a household name. A genius both with the sword and the stylus, Caesar also, according to Cicero, was an eloquent and persuasive orator. (Fields-Carré Collection)

Whereas Pompey was glorified by the Greek intelligentsia around him, the great man himself being somewhat ill at ease with the pen, Caesar was now glorified by his own clear Latin. 'Avoid an unfamiliar word', he used to say, 'as a sailor avoids the rocks' (Aulus Gellius *Noctes Atticae* 1.10.4), and it has been calculated that Caesar employed a 1,300-word vocabulary virtually cleansed of colloquial corruptions and foreign coinages (Welch-Powell, 1998: 21). Elegantly and lucidly written in the third person, which allows him to write his name 775 times, no figure naturally casts a greater shadow in his *commentarii* than Caesar, and he styled himself in what we would now a brand. With or without Shakespeare, Caesar (as seen by Caesar) would have lived in history because, quite simply, he decided that it should be so.

In fact the *Bellum Gallicum* was never destined to become a dusty museum piece, and so Caesar's ambition came to fruition. Yet we must constantly bear in mind that his practical military experience before he went to Gaul had been minimal. It had included a fascinating, private encounter with pirates as a young man (75 BC) and a short participation as a junior officer in Asia and Cilicia (Second Mithridatic War, 83–81 BC), where he was to win Rome's highest decoration, the *corona civica*, for saving the life of a fellow soldier at the storming of Mytilene (81 BC). It is possible he saw some action as a military tribune sometime during the Spartacan War (73–71 BC), perhaps under Crassus himself. Also, a few years before his Gallic command, he had tasted tribal warfare first hand as propraetor in Iberia (61–60 BC).

It is said that it is not by blood that man's true continuity is established, and, if the truth be told, Alexander's direct military successor was the great Pompey, glorious from victories in all quarters of the world, not Caesar, destroyer of Gaul. Yet the Gallic campaigns were to Caesar a hard-knock school of war, an arena in which he could learn his trade and his army be disciplined and toughened. At the end of his ten-year tenure in Gaul, Caesar was a cool and daring commander of a highly efficient and fanatically loyal army.

THE EARLY YEARS

Caesar married Cornelia, daughter of the Republic's supremo Cinna, and they had a daughter, Iulia, named after his paternal aunt, the wife of Marius, the same Marius who had reorganized the army and led it to a string of celebrated victories in Africa and Gaul. When Sulla marched on Rome for a second time and became its dictator, a long-obsolete emergency magistracy that he revived, he ordered the 18-year-old Caesar to divorce Cornelia as a demonstration of loyalty to the new warlord of the Republic. Caesar refused. Sulla was impressed with his courage and spared him, saying, 'In this young man there is more than one Marius' (Plutarch *Caesar* 1.2). If the story is true, then Sulla must have been a remarkably good judge of character.

Caesar had been born in 100 BC, the sixth consulship of Marius. A few months before the birth, Marius had enjoyed the almost superhuman glory of his second triumph, that over the Cimbri and the Teutones. The ancestral bust in the atrium of the Iulii included ten consuls, but eight of those had been in the dim and distant days of the 5th century BC, and there was only one with a triumphal garland, Caesar's great-great-great-great-grandfather, victor in some forgotten skirmish near Brundisium in 267 BC. Thus the family had only managed to produce a single consul during the entire 2nd century BC, at the height of Rome's overseas expansion. At the time the marriage connection with Marius was worth more to the family than its own record, and may be the reason for its revival, marked by the Iulii consuls (Caesar's uncle and two of his cousins) of 91, 90 and 64 BC.

In most respects his early career was conventional, unlike that of Pompey, and it would be erroneous of us to insist (as his Greek biographer Plutarch does) that Caesar began his ascent to power and glory with a well-orchestrated plan for achieving supremacy in Rome. It was not quite that simple – history seldom is. Still,

Caesar is said to have had an affair with Nikomedes of Bithynia while serving as Rome's envoy to the king's court in Prusa (81 BC). This adventure earned for him the unflattering title 'Queen of Bithynia'. Renamed Bursa by the Ottomans, the city served as their first capital (1326). South façade of Koza Hanı (1451), the silk cocoon *han*. (Fields-Carré Collection)

there is no doubt that Caesar was keenly aware of just how to capitalize on any action that could increase his prestige. This is clear early in his political career, in 69 BC – long before his successes in Gaul – during the funeral of his aunt Iulia. Roman funerals were understood as an occasion to honour both the deceased and the greatness of the family. Funerals were held for the living more so than the dead. And so the occasion prompted Caesar to make the first attempt at becoming the leader of the *populares* ('radicals' or – to their opponents – 'demagogues') that in

the past had followed Marius. Sulla had been safely dead for ten years by this time, but his followers, *optimates* (the 'good men') in the main, still controlled Rome, and, after all, the dictator's entire political programme had been an attempt to scotch the *populares* tradition and uphold the entrenched power and privilege of the senatorial oligarchy. In her funeral procession Caesar displayed, besides the images of other members of the family, the image of his deceased uncle Marius, the husband of Iulia and Sulla's greatest foe.

Displaying images of relatives was common, but displaying Marius' image was daring and dangerous, because the state had forbidden it. Thus Caesar's action was a deliberate challenge to some of the powerful Roman families that had sided with Sulla. His action was criticized but not punished. Four years later, as aedile, he would surreptitiously replace the trophies of Marius on the Capitol, and again survived the attack of the Sullan faction and became the spokesman and leader of the Marians, who favoured his conduct. When he began to display images of Marius, long a nonperson, no mention was made in the accompanying inscriptions of his uncle's triumph in Africa but rather of his victories over Rome's most serious threat in recent times – the Cimbri and the Teutones. 'And all who saw them were amazed at the daring of man who had set them up – it was quite obvious who he was' (Plutarch *Caesar* 6.2). He would prove to be the most masterly *populares* in Roman politics, yet by birth he was a true patrician, descended from the oldest nobility in Roman history. For the Iulii claimed descent from the legendary kings of Alba Longa, and through them from the founding father Aeneas of Troy, whose mother was the goddess Venus and whose son Iulus originated the family name. In every society the aristocracy have been those who can trace their ancestors back a long way, for obvious reasons that this is the yardstick of having held positions of power for a long time. It is a delightful game if you happen to be an aristocrat, and one which Caesar, with his esteemed ancestry and moral virtue, played superbly.

Since the Romans believed that Aeneas, son of Venus, was their forefather, his son Iulus having founded Alba Longa, they attached great importance to Troy. Caesar, who traced his ancestry back to Iulus, offered sacrifices at the temple of Athena during a visit to Troy en route to Egypt after Pharsalus. These scattered marble architectural elements are all that remain of the temple. (Fields-Carré Collection)

According to Suetonius (*DI* 2.2), history first took notice of the young Caesar when he 'won his spurs' during the Roman storming of Mytilene (81 BC), then occupied by troops of Mithridates. A general view of Mytilene town – now dominated by the ruins of a Genoese castle (1374) – looking east from the old port. (Fields-Carré Collection)

So as to perfect his oratory skills, Caesar left Italy in 75 BC to study rhetoric at Rhodes under the renowned maestro Apollonios, the son of Molon. However, en route to the island he was snatched by a band of pirates. General view of Rhodes town looking south-west towards the Fort Saint Nicolas (1464), a cylindrical tower built by the Knights Hospitaller. (Fields-Carré Collection)

Fear was not part of Caesar's character. Back in 75 BC, whilst on a ship bound for Rhodes, he had been captured by Cilician pirates. They put a ransom of 20 talents on his head, an enormous sum, but Caesar thought this was too small and insolently informed them that he was worth at least 50. The pirates had a good laugh and let a few of his companions go in order to secure the ransom money. Meantime Caesar treated the pirates as if they were his personal bodyguard, ordering them around and leaving no doubt as to who was in charge. They played along and went on laughing even when he told them that after his release he would come back to take revenge. As soon as the ransom was paid, Caesar was set ashore. He immediately went to Miletos, put together a small fleet and went back and did exactly what he said he was going to do. Every pirate he was able to catch was to suffer the frightful Roman punishment of crucifixion. But because they had treated him well during his captivity, he had their throats slit before they were put on the cross, a token of compassion (*DI* 74).

The functionaries known as aediles sought to attract popularity by giving *ludi honorarii*, supplementary games attached to theatre and circus performances. Aediles supervised the public life of Rome at street level, and they soon learned that they could manipulate their office to improve their chances of being elected to more senior magistracies in future years. The funds provided by the state could be used by the aediles to put on adequate

public festivals, but to make a real impression they had to dip into their own purses. Such games could be very costly and, being free to the public, there was no profit to be made. So the investment was high risk, and many found themselves almost bankrupt by their year in office, but if a man went on to hold one of the more senior (and lucrative) political posts he would be able to recoup his investment and repay any money he had borrowed. It was as one of the aediles of 65 BC, writes Suetonius, that Caesar, in honour of his father who had been dead for 20 years, put on a gladiatorial show: 'but he collected so immense a troop of combatants that his terrified political opponents rushed a bill through the Senate, limiting the number that anyone might keep in Rome; consequently far fewer pairs fought than had been advertised' (*DI* 10.2). Caesar was undaunted. He made certain everyone in Rome knew that it was the Senate that had robbed them of the most spectacular games of all time. All the same his diminished troupe of gladiators still amounted to 320 pairs, and each man was equipped with armour specially made from solid silver.

Caesar's show was not only a huge success but also hugely expensive. For money Caesar had turned to Marcus Licinius Crassus. It had been Crassus who had crushed bloodily the rebellion of Spartacus, but it had been Pompey who had stolen most of the credit. Magnificent Pompey was currently in the east earning more glory for himself but would soon be back in the political arena of Rome. Crassus was therefore willing to use some of his stupendous wealth in furthering the career of a potential rival to Pompey. As Sallust says, 'Crassus, it was thought, would have been glad to see Pompey's supremacy threatened by the rise of another powerful man, whoever he might be' (*Bellum Catilinae* 17.7).

The post of chief priest, *pontifex maximus,* became vacant in 63 BC with the death of Quintus Caecilius Metellus Pius (*cos.* 80 BC), Pompey's colleague

Caesar visits the Temple of Hercules (1894), oil painting by Godoy. We know that while serving as quaestor in Hispania Ulterior (69 BC) he visited such a shrine in Gades. It was there, according to Suetonius, that Caesar gazed upon a statue of Alexander and sighed that at his age 'Alexander had already conquered the whole world' (*DI* 7). Fact or fable? (Ancient art & Architecture)

of the Sertorian War (79–72 BC). As the highest of all priests responsible for overseeing the official auguries of the priests and magistrates at Rome, this office was the crown of a distinguished career. It was given, therefore, to retired censors and well-regarded *consulares*, illustrious men, in fact, like the senior conservative *nobilis* Quintus Lutatius Catulus (*cos.* 78 BC) the son of Marius' campaigning colleague in the northern war and the favoured candidate. Caesar, who had risen no further than aedile, had the temerity to stand against him. On the morning of the election, Caesar kissed his mother goodbye with the remark: 'Today, Mother, you will see your son either as *pontifex maximus* or as an exile' (Plutarch *Caesar* 7.2). Plausibly, as Suetonius' version has it (*DI* 13), the electors were bribed on a monstrous scale and thus Caesar was successful. He held this very honourable position until his death.

Caesar, neoclassical statue (Paris, musée du Louvre, MR 1798) by Nicolas Coustou (1658–1733). Commissioned in 1696 for the parc de Versailles (to stand alongside the *Hannibal* by Sébastien Slodtz), its bearing (and baton) is somewhat reminiscent of *le roi soleil*, Louis XIV. King of France and warlord for more than 70 years, Louis led his armies in his youth but, unlike Caesar, never fought a major battle. (Fields-Carré Collection)

THE MILITARY LIFE

In 69 BC Caesar had served as quaestor in Hispania Ulterior, but this tour of duty disappointed him since it offered no opportunity for glory, and he soon returned to Rome. However, six years later he was to return as propraetor. The Senate granted this appointment in order to counteract the Lusitani, a people of western Iberia who had been subdued by Pompey during the Sertorian War but who were now raiding Roman settlements in the peninsula. It seems Caesar was determined to use this situation to further his political career at home, and also to gain enough wealth to clear the massive debts that he had incurred. In a series of wide-ranging expeditions he won several engagements against the dissident tribesmen and established Roman authority as far as the Atlantic. Having stabilized the situation, he now thrust northwards. Using the fleet stationed in Gades (Cádiz) in support, he reached the extreme north-west and took the chief settlement of the Callaeici, Brigantium (La Coruña).

For these highly successful policing operations along the Atlantic seaboard, Caesar earned for himself a triumph. The problem was he also wanted to stand for the consulship of 59 BC, and in order to be eligible the candidate had to submit his name personally and thus enter Rome, namely cross the *pomoerium*, a virtual sacred boundary. Unfortunately for Caesar, the law stated that a victorious general awaiting his triumph had to remain outside the city limits with his soldiers until granted permission to retain his power, in Caesar's case *imperium pro praetore*, within the city on the day of his triumph. Indeed, it was among the most essential provisions of the Roman constitution that no army should ever be brought into Rome, and that a general must lay aside his command (and the legal immunity it gave him) before entering the city.

In order not to forfeit his triumph, according to Plutarch (*Cato minor* 31.2–3), Caesar asked the Senate for permission to register *in absentia*. Many of the senators were willing to consent to it, but Marcus Porcius Cato, Caesar's bitterest political foe, opposed it. A decision had to be reached before nightfall on a certain day. On the last day remaining before the election lists closed, Cato employed his favourite tactic of filibustering, haranguing his colleagues in his booming, rasping voice until the sun went down. Rough and unadorned, the voice of Cato appeared to sound directly from the rugged, virtuous days of a bygone Rome. Cicero, who admired Cato deeply, could nevertheless bitch that 'he addresses the Senate as though he were living in Plato's Republic rather than Romulus' cesspool' (*Ad Att.* 2.1.6). Whatever, the very next morning Caesar coolly laid aside his command, thereby giving up his triumph, and entered Rome to seek election, his honour dented. Yet the sacrifice of a once-in-a-lifetime triumph gives an indication of just how confident he was of gaining the highest of offices.

Every consul, once he had completed his term of office, was appointed to a governorship as a matter of course. The Senate, according to Suetonius, so as to limit his influence, awarded Caesar not Iberia or Gaul but the humdrum provincial command of 'woods and drove roads' (*DI* 19.2) in Italy itself, which was normally the task of a praetor. Suetonius obviously presents this as a deliberate insult to Caesar. It has been suggested that as the Gallic tribes were once again on the move the Senate wanted to keep one proconsul in Italy, stressing the fact that Caesar did gain his Gallic command later that same year. However, it does appear that this was a definite political ploy by the *optimates* to prevent Caesar taking up a major overseas command.

The clear-sighted Caesar was quick to realize that there was an interesting possibility at hand. His plan was to be brutally simple: to carry Pompey and Crassus with him in a mutual balance of favours. Caesar had lost his triumph, Pompey a land bill to settle his veterans and Crassus had been snubbed over a recent government contract, all through the machinations of Cato and the *optimates*. Crassus had the money, Pompey the soldiers and Caesar the backing of the people. Caesar therefore argued that the three of them should come together and pool their resources and thereby turn the tables on the

Legionaries on the Altar of Domitius Ahenobarbus (Paris, musée du Louvre, Ma 975). In the warfare waged by Caesar his special instrument was the army that, as he himself claimed, could storm the very heavens with or without him (Anon. *Bellum Hispaniense* 42.6). Here, in the mingling of the souls of Caesar and his legions, was the glimpse of a new order. (Fields-Carré Collection)

Marble bust (Vienna, Kunsthistorisches Museum) of a grim-looking Caesar. During his campaigns in Gaul his manner of waging warfare was to conquer either by physical violence or by psychological persuasion. War then as now was Janus-faced: fight a war of the mind as much as a war of blood and iron; pay off the passive; pacify the proud. (Andrew Bossi)

opposition by forming a faction. Pompey, who had wanted to become Cato's son-in-law, became Caesar's instead, marrying Caesar's beloved only daughter, Iulia. And so the alliance was cemented.

We should understand that the triumvirate had no legal authority under the constitution and that its aims were short term. The terms of the political liaison were quite precise; Caesar would use his consulship to steamroller through a package of laws in the interests of all three, legislation that had been held up by Cato and his clique. Once this had been achieved there was no real reason to keep the coalition together, and as such it worked effectively. Pompey got the land for his veterans 'with no opposition' (Cassius Dio 38.7.5). Pompey had brought his veterans – the very men who would benefit from the bill granting land – into the city, a tacit threat to anyone inclined to oppose the measure. Crassus was able to secure recompense for his business associates, who in turn 'extolled Caesar to the skies' (Appian *Bellum civilia* 2.13).

Having fulfilled his obligations toward his two colleagues, Caesar set about consolidating his own constitutional position and preparing for his proconsulship. To this end he had himself allocated to the governorship of Illyricum and Gallia Cisalpina (what is now the Adriatic Balkan coast and Italy north of the Po). The addition of Gallia Transalpina was a fortunate stroke of luck following the sudden death of the allotted governor. His enemies may have believed that his growing reputation would be buried in the barbarous lands beyond the Alps, and he would in any case be far removed from the central arena. But Caesar saw his appointment as a capital chance for political advancement, for it gave him the power not only to raise troops, but also to gain victories, which might rival those of the gloriously endowed Pompey, and to amass a fortune, which he badly needed to break his dependence on the notoriously wealthy Crassus. Succeeding in politics, much like today, was a wickedly expensive business, and the proconsulship was set to last until some (apparently unspecified) time in 54 BC (later extended for a further five years in 55 BC).

His fellow Romans would have referred to the distant land of Gaul as Gallia Comata (long-haired Gaul), while the south-eastern part was usually referred to by Caesar as Provincia, the Province. Its official name was Gallia Transalpina (Gaul-across-the-Alps) in contrast to Gallia Cisalpina (Gaul-this-side-of-the-Alps). In the Italian Peninsula the Rubicon marked the boundary between Gallia Cisalpina and Italy proper. Gallia Transalpina, unlike Gallia Comata, was already part of the empire. It had come under Roman control in the 2nd century BC, following the development of Roman links with Greek Massilia (Marseilles), and the establishment of a permanent fortified outpost at Aquae Sextiae (Aix-en-Provence), the site of Marius' victory against the Teutones in 102 BC. Gallia Transalpina gave the Romans an important land route from Italy to Iberia, where Roman influence had been much longer established.

The control of this route, along which successive Roman armies passed, and the safeguarding of Roman economic interests were thus a major

Caesar's campaigns, Gallic War (58–51 BC) and Civil War (49–45 BC)

CASPIAN SEA

ATROPATENE

ALBANI

IBERIA

ARMENIA

COLCHIS

PARTHIA

Tigris

Euphrates

PONTUS

Zela 47 BC

CAPPADOCIA

COMMAGENE

GALATIA

EMESA

ITURAEA

JUDAEA

NABATAEA

RED SEA

Nile

BOSPORUS

BLACK SEA

PAPHLAGONIA

Alexandria 48 BC

PTOLEMAIC KINGDOM

DACIA

Danubius

AEGEAN SEA

Pharsalus 48 BC

Dyrrhachium 48 BC

Brundisium 49 BC

IONIAN SEA

Corfinium 49 BC

ADRIATIC SEA

MEDITERRANEAN SEA

Padus

TYRRHENIAN SEA

Thapsus 46 BC

Rhenus

Rhodanus

Sequana

Ilerda 49 BC

Iberus

Durius

Munda 45 BC

ATLANTIC OCEAN

N

MAURETANIA

Limits of direct Roman rule on death of Caesar, 44 BC

Client kingdom

Site of major engagement (with date)

0   500 miles
0   500km

Caesar's Gallic Campaigns, 58–51 BC

GERMANIA

Rhenus

55 53

HELVETII

58

GALLIA CISALPINA

Rhodanus

55

55

NERVII 57 54

EBURONES

BELGAE

52

Alesia

52

Gergovia

58

58

Lugdunum

Aquae Sextiae (Aix-en-Provence)

Massilia (Marseille)

BRITANNIA

54

Sequana

GAULS

Agedincum

Liger

52

Avaricum

52

Bibracte

52

58

TRANSALPINA

GALLIA TRANSALPINA

Narbo (Narbonne)

MEDITERRANEAN SEA

ENGLISH CHANNEL

56

VENETI

56

51

Uxello-dunum

AQUITANI

56

Tolosa (Toulouse)

Garunna

Iberus

ATLANTIC OCEAN

13

concern to the Senate. Cicero could write 'all Gaul is filled with Italian traders, all Provincia is full of Roman citizens' (*De re publica* 3.16), an exaggeration no doubt, but when the stability of Gaul was threatened by the migration of the Helvetii and the political machinations of the Germanic war leader Ariovistus, Caesar was provided with an admirable excuse to move his legions deep into uncharted territory.

Caesar's uncle had saved Italy from the threatened invasion of the Cimbri and the Teutones, whose victories inflicted on earlier Roman commanders echo ominously in the background of the *commentarii*, but the vivid memory of the near disaster remained. Barbarian migrations were the stuff of Roman nightmares, and Caesar made good use of it by playing up the 'Germanic menace'. His assessment of the Gallic political scene – Gaul would have to become Roman or it would be overrun by the fierce warlike Germanic race – was probably a gross hyperbole, but as a justification for his Gallic campaigns it would have convinced many who remembered the panic of five decades before.

The forces available to Caesar, when he arrived in Gallia Cisalpina, consisted of three legions, numbered in orderly sequence from *VII* to *VIIII*, with a further legion, *X*, in Gallia Transalpina. He also raised from scratch two legions (*XI* and *XII*) in Italy. These six legions were supported by an unspecified number of auxiliaries, including Iberian horsemen, Numidian javelineers and perhaps also horsemen, Cretan archers and Balearic slingers, along with a number of locally raised Gallic troops, horsemen in the main. We know nothing about the previous history of Caesar's legions, except that they were already in his provinces when he took up his command. Under the legislation appointing him to the command, he was allowed a quaestor to handle the financial affairs of the provinces, and ten legates whom he could appoint directly, without reference to the Senate.

Striking bust (Berlin, Altes Museum), most likely of Caesar, carved some 50 years after his murder from green basanite, an igneous volcanic stone from Wadi Hamamat, Upper Egypt. Caesar is perhaps the best known of all the Romans, his name transmitted into later European history as *kaiser* and *czar*. It was also incorporated into the occidental calendar as the month of July. (Ancient Art & Architecture)

THE HOUR OF DESTINY

Caesar, like Alexander before him, would gain his reputation by seeking out the enemy, bringing him to a set-piece battle, and annihilating him. To achieve this comfortably he had to exercise control over his army at all times, being close enough to read the battle without getting involved in the initial fight. Therefore, during an action, Caesar, unlike Alexander, rode about close behind the front line of his army. From this sensible position he encouraged his men, witnessed their behaviour and rewarded or punished them accordingly. He also had a close view of the combat zone and could appreciate the situation as the thousands battled, judging the fight by the morale exhibited and the yells made by friend and foe alike. Using this information he could feed in reinforcements from his second or third lines to exploit a success or relieve part of the fighting line that was under pressure. Put simply, Caesar had tactical *coup d'oeil*, that is to say, the ability

Gilded silver cauldron (Copenhagen, Nationalmuseet), discovered by peat cutters at Gundestrop, Jutland (1891). Dismantled and deposited in a peat bog as a votive offering, it was probably made in the Balkans some time during the late 2nd century BC. One of the inside panels shows a procession of Celtic horsemen, who provided the highest quality troops in any Celtic army. They were drawn chiefly from the nobles – the *equites* mentioned by Caesar. (Malene Thyssen)

to perceive the decisive point, even the need to intervene personally in the fight when his army was on the verge of defeat or when the moment had arrived to move in for the kill. That personal intervention on the battlefield was not considered incompatible with the demands of leadership can be seen from Caesar's praise (*BG* 5.33.2) of the doomed Lucius Aurunculeius Cotta for fulfilling the duties of a commander and fighting in the ranks as a common soldier.

Just as the function of a soldier was to fight battles, the function of a commander was to win battles. He therefore needed to judge where and when the crisis of battle would occur and move to that part of the fighting line, and there is no doubt that in this function Caesar took up such a prudent position to ensure he reacted positively and instinctively. At one point during his blockade of Dyrrhachium, Caesar had placed Publius Cornelius Sulla in temporary command. When the legate was informed of an assault on one of the redoubts, held by a lone cohort, he rushed to its support with two legions and repulsed the Pompeians, and, when his men hared off in pursuit, he recalled them and was censored for doing so. But on his return Caesar judged Sulla to have acted rightly, for, as he says, 'the duties of a legate and of a commander are different: the one ought to do everything under direction, the other should take measures freely in the general interest' (*BC* 3.51.6). Like Napoleon after him, Caesar chafed at independent action. This was the chief's prerogative. He took sole control of the army, deciding what is what, directing the soldiers and directing their blades. Such is the work of the commander. Bearing a single sword is not a commander's affair.

Having said all that, often we find Caesar next to his soldiers, exposing life and limb to mortal danger. Even in his first major engagement, he sent away his and his officers' horses as a grand gesture to his men that he was personally committed to battle and neither could nor would save his own skin (*BG* 1.25.1). Caesar understood his soldiers as few did, with the probable exception of his uncle Marius. He shared with them the glories, the rewards, but also the toils, miseries and, above all, the dangers of soldiering. He was indifferent to personal comforts or luxuries and since boyhood had been an expert horseman who had even trained himself to ride at full gallop with both hands clasped behind his back. During the campaigns in Gaul he even got into the habit of dictating dispatches while on horseback. If Caesar was a risk taker, he was one who carefully hedged his bets: if he stepped into a fight, the decision was taken either by necessity or by the certainty that the risk was small and the promise of reward great. In a breathless tête-à-tête on the banks of the Sabis Caesar's army was caught totally unprepared while making camp and it would be his splendid example of bravery that would help save the day. At Alesia, in contrast, he led the final attack as the enemy was on the verge of collapse, and when his soldiers realized that Caesar himself was coming, they fought with greater vigour. Anyway, before analyzing Caesar's generalship, we shall look at some of his battles.

The battle of the Sabis

By 57 BC it had become clear that Caesar had decided on the total conquest of Gaul. Raising a further two legions (*XIII* and *XIIII*), Caesar turned his attention to the subjugation of the Belgae, a loose confederation of tribes who occupied the territory north of the Sequana (Seine). Some of them were settled on the North Sea littoral, and significant groups had been crossing to Britannia for several generations and establishing kingdoms there. Having beaten a substantial Belgic army near Bibrax (either Beaurieux or Vieux Laon) in the

Battle of the Sabis, summer 57 BC

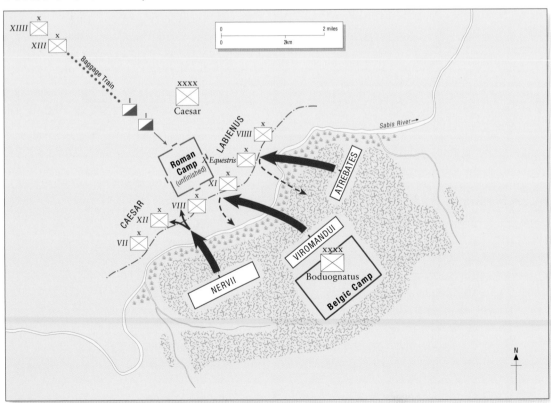

territory of the Remi, Caesar quickly moved northwards against the more remote Belgic tribes, among them the Nervii, a fierce warrior people who proclaimed they would rather accept death than Roman domination.

With two legions still en route, the other six legions were entrenching their camp for the night on rising ground above the Sabis (Sambre), when the enemy charged out of the marshland and forest some 300m (330 yards) on the other side of the river, crossed it, and raced up the slopes towards them with incredible speed. According to Caesar, and the following account is very much based upon that given by him in his second *commentarius*, his army faced at least 60,000 warriors of the Nervii, along with the Atrebates and Viromandui. Whatever the actual numbers may have been, they outnumbered Caesar's 40,000 legionaries.

Almost wrong footed by this sudden attack, the legionaries dropped their entrenching tools, grabbed their arms and automatically created a line-of-battle by falling in around the nearest standard instead of seeking their own cohorts. Thus a ragged improvised battle line was formed, with *legiones VIIII* and *X Equestris* holding the left, *legiones VIII* and *XI* the centre, and *legiones VII* and *XII* the right. Opposite them the Nervii created a very strong left wing, the Viromandui held the centre, and the Atrebates the right. The two cavalry forces were already hotly engaged, with the Gauls mauling the Roman auxiliaries, many of them Gauls themselves.

Despite the battle line being cut up by the broken terrain, the legionaries held fast and withstood the Belgic onslaught. The Roman centre and left were successful, the latter driving the Atrebates pell-mell down the slope and across the Sabis, and then chasing them up the rising ground on its far side. However, this success left the half-built Roman camp and the right wing of their battle line exposed and some of the Nervii overran the camp and took the baggage train.

In the meantime, the bulk of the Nervii had outflanked the Roman right. Ideally the tremendous punch the Roman Army delivered in battle came from the legionaries, but here they were in great difficulties as most of their centurions had been killed or injured and their ranks had become too packed together to allow them to operate effectively. The situation was critical. But Caesar, unfazed, wrung every advantage from his position. He dismounted and grabbed a *scutum* from a man in the rear, then made his way to the forefront of the fighting line, yelling orders for the ranks and files to open so that the legionaries, instinctively huddled together to resist the flood of the Nervii and giving way under pressure, might be able to bring as many blades as possible into the fray and consequently demoralize the opposition. And so it came to pass, for as soon as warriors in the foremost ranks fell under the blows of the legionaries, there was a halt and then a falling back. Following an attack from the rear, and a scrimmage, the defeat of the Nervii ensued.

The nitty-gritty of tactics is to make men fight with their maximum vigour, and discipline is the cornerstone of tactics. The Romans excelled the Gauls in

Reverse of *denarius* (London, British Museum) bearing a head of a captive Gaul, dated to 48 BC. The Gauls had a fearsome reputation for aggressiveness, even among the militaristic Romans, who, initially, were terrified by these wild, larger-than-life northerners, who bore long iron swords, adorned themselves with gold torques, wore long moustaches and hair that was slaked with lime to make it stand up like a horse's mane. (PHGCOM)

Inner circle: Caesar before Alesia

Although there was still no permanent legionary commander, and this situation would remain so until the establishment of the Principate under Augustus, there were still, as in the days of Marius, six military tribunes, *tribuni militum*, in each legion. Likewise, tribunes were still elected by the citizens in the *comitia centuriata*, as was the young Caesar (Plutarch *Caesar* 5.1). On the other hand, additional tribunes could be chosen by a general himself. Here demands of *amicitiae* were met by taking on to his staff family, friends, and the sons of political associates, who were thus able to acquire some military service and experience that would stand them in good stead for their future excursion into politics. Cicero's friend Caius Trebatius was offered a tribunate by Caesar (*Ad fam.* 7.5.3, 8.1), and for a young inexperienced blue blood such an appointment was the swiftest way of kick starting a political career, the *cursus honorum*.

However, there is no instance of a tribune commanding a legion in action during Caesar's campaigns in Gaul. As they were invariably short-term politicos, who had an eye cast in the direction of Rome, tribunes could be rather an embarrassment at times. In their place Caesar started to appoint a senior officer, usually a legate (*legatus*, pl. *legati*), both for the command of individual legions and as a commander of an expeditionary force detached from the main army. Usually of senatorial rank, some of these men might be former proconsular governors or army commanders, providing the leadership, experience and stability that the legion needed to operate effectively. In Gaul the most prominent of these legates was Titus Atius Labienus, Caesar's second-in-command as a *legatus pro praetore* ('subordinate officer acting in place of a praetor'), who at times was employed as an independent army commander, and who commanded the entire army in Caesar's absence. During the conflict between Caesar and Pompey, we will find Labienus on the other side once battle was joined. Another of Caesar's legates at Alesia was Marcus Antonius.

Yet in his *commentarii* the centurions are the true heroes. They were a tough, hand-picked body of men of great dependability and courage. Referring to those celebrated rivals Titus Pullo and Lucius Vorenus, who vied with each other in exhibiting bravery, Caesar says the two centurions were 'close to entering the *primi ordines*' (*BG* 5.44.1). The six centurions of the first cohort were collectively known as the *primi ordines* ('front rankers') and enjoyed immense prestige. Centurions *primorum ordinum* are coupled by Caesar with the tribunes and were regarded as members of the councils of war he regularly held with his legates.

Wise commanders recognized the value of their centurions not only in leading men into battle, but also in providing valuable advice based on their experience of war. Caesar himself would have listened to their views and used them to pass on information and orders to the rank and file. Their understanding of an intended battle plan was vital for success simply because they were the ones leading the men on the ground. Centurions were the key to an army's success in battle, and Caesar knew it.

Here Caesar is in his command tent holding a council of war. Caesar (1) himself is listening to the views of some his 'front rankers' (2). In the background stand Labienus (3) and Antonius (4).

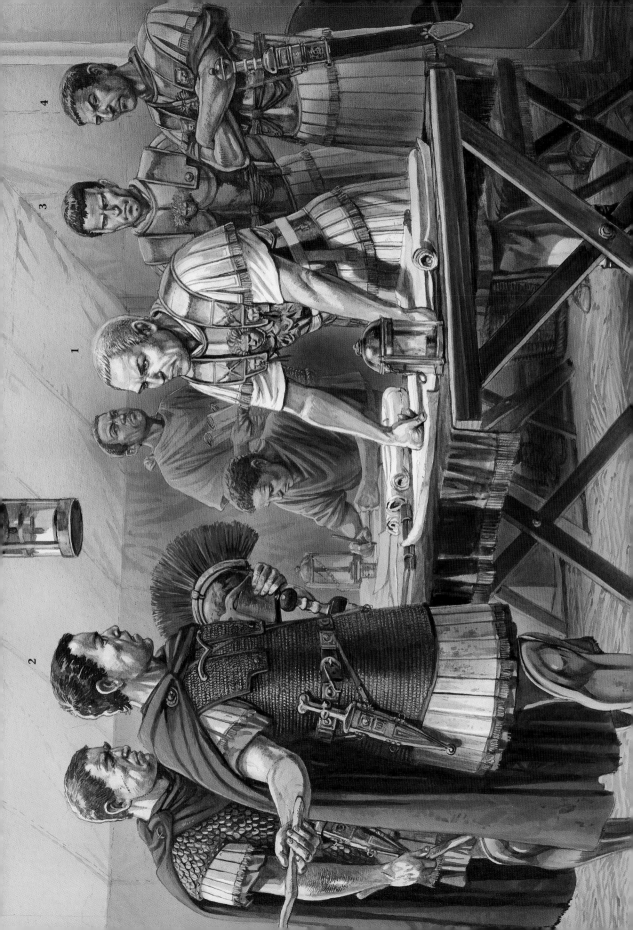

this, though not in bravery. The Gauls fought in war bands that were fragile, virtually clouds of individuals. They were almost as much in competition with each other for glory as in conflict with the foe, rushing in and swinging slashing swords of iron, intent on reducing shields to matchwood and men to pulp. Roman discipline, on the other hand, demanded doggedness. The hardening of the men to fatigue, and a good organization, giving mutual support, produced that doggedness, against which the bravest could not stand. Besides, the exhausting method of powerful strokes employed by the Gauls, albeit red-blooded and strongly limbed, could not last long against the skilful and less fatiguing method of swordplay utilizing the thrust.

Caesar's overconfidence had led to a near disaster, but his energetic reaction and presence on foot helped to stiffen resistance. The Nervii, who refused to surrender or retreat, were annhilated. This significant victory broke the power of the Belgae to such an extent that even Germanic tribes beyond the Rhenus (Rhine) sent envoys to Caesar offering submission.

The siege of Alesia

By the close of 53 BC Caesar had increased his army to ten legions with the formation of two units (*XIIII* and *XV*, the former replacing the 'lost' *XIIII*) and the borrowing of another, *legio I*, from Pompey (part of his consular series in 55 BC). During the winter of 53–52 BC Caesar enrolled non-citizen soldiers in Gallia Transalpina, the genesis of *legio V Alaudae* – in theory, Roman citizens alone were eligible for legionary service – with another legion, numbered *VI*, being brought into service a little later.

In his seventh *commentarius* Caesar himself narrates at some length his operations at the foot of Alesia (Alise-Sainte-Reine). The *oppidum* sat atop an oval mesa-like hill (Mont Auxois, 406m) with a flat top that fell off precipitously, plunging perpendicularly for some 50m (160ft), while the

Section of Caesar's siegeworks at Alesia, reconstructed at Beaune. Here we see the camouflaged pitfalls, beyond which lie the double ditches and earthworks (constructed in concrete) crowned with a timber palisade. Forked branches are embedded in the earthworks, while towers overlook the defences. The original ran for 11 Roman miles, with a corresponding line of circumvallation of 14 Roman miles. (Ancient Art & Architecture)

plateau topside was 2km (1 mile) long and 600m (650 yards) wide. Running east to west north and south of the *oppidum* were the Oze and Ozerain rivers. To the west of the hill the two river valleys merged to form a broad plain. Vercingetorix had a trench dug on either side of the hill, making an approach to the *oppidum* almost as difficult an assault, and fortified the surrounding plateau with a rough-built wall 6 Roman feet (1.78m) high, a virtual vertical extension of the sheer part of the hillside. With his 80,000 warriors and 1,500 horsemen, Vercingetorix believed Alesia was unassailable.

Commanding less than 50,000 legionaries and assorted auxiliaries, Caesar nevertheless opened the siege. Having analyzed the site and judged its difficulties, Alesia seemed more difficult to defend than to lay siege to. Vercingetorix despatched his cavalry to rally reinforcements from across Gaul, and in turn Caesar constructed a contravallation and circumvallation, an elaborate siege work that stretched for a total of 25 Roman miles (37km) and linked an encircling chain of 23 forts and eight camps. The siege lines themselves consisted of a sheer-sided trench 20 Roman feet (5.92m) wide across the plain at the western foot of the hill to protect the men working on the contravallation 400 Roman paces behind this and facing inwards towards Alesia. This consisted of two ditches each 15 Roman feet (4.44m) wide and 8 Roman feet (2.37m) deep covered by an earthwork and palisade, 12 Roman

Siege of Alesia, summer 52 BC

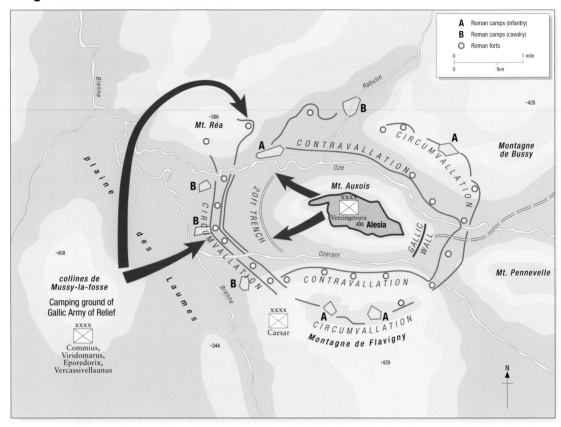

feet (3.55m) in overall height and studded with timber observation towers every 80 Roman feet (23.67m). Forked branches (*cervi*) were embedded in the top of the earthwork so that they projected horizontally to prevent any attempt to scale it.

To slow the approach of any daylight assault and to disrupt any night foray mounted by the besieged Gauls, the Romans devised more elaborate obstacles, camouflaged circular pits in checkerboard formation concealing sharp fire-hardened stakes, ironically nicknamed by the soldiers *lilia* ('lilies'), interspersed with *stimuli* ('stingers'), foot-long logs with iron spikes embedded in them. Between these booby traps and the two ditches were *cippi* ('boundary markers'), five rows of sharpened branches, fixed in channels 5 Roman feet (1.48m) deep and interlaced to form a hedge of spikes. A parallel line of defences and obstacles was then provided as a circumvallation against the inevitable Gallic relief army.

When this relief army arrived, the Romans faced the warriors in Alesia plus an alleged 250,000 warriors and 8,000 horsemen attacking from without. Caesar adroitly employed his interior lines, his fortifications and the greater training and discipline of his men to offset the Gallic advantage, but after two days of heavy fighting his army was pressed to the breaking point. On the third day the Gauls, equipped with fascines, scaling ladders and grappling hooks, captured the north-western angle of the circumvallation (Mont Réa, 386m), which formed a crucial point in the Roman defences. In desperation, Caesar personally led the last of his reserves in a do-or-die counterattack, and, when his Germanic horsemen outflanked the Gauls and took them in the rear, the battle decisively turned to his advantage. With the relief force shattered and food supplies in Alesia almost exhausted, Vercingetorix surrendered the following day.

The battle of Pharsalus

Caesar himself never mentions Pharsalus, the most famous engagement of the civil war. In fact, in his whole narrative of events immediately preceding and following the battle, and the battle itself, he mentions no place at all except Larissa (Lárissa). Such topographical information as is given in his account and in other sources is of little help in identifying the exact location of the battlefield.

While Appian, Plutarch and Suetonius refer to 'the battle of Pharsalus', Frontinus, Eutropius, Orosius and the author of the *Bellum Alexandrinum*, believed by many to be the soldier-scholar Aulus Hirtius, give the additional detail that it was fought somewhere near 'Old Pharsalus', a stronghold on a hill in the territory of Pharsalus proper. Pharsalus is generally agreed to be

Battle of Pharsalus, 9 August 48 BC

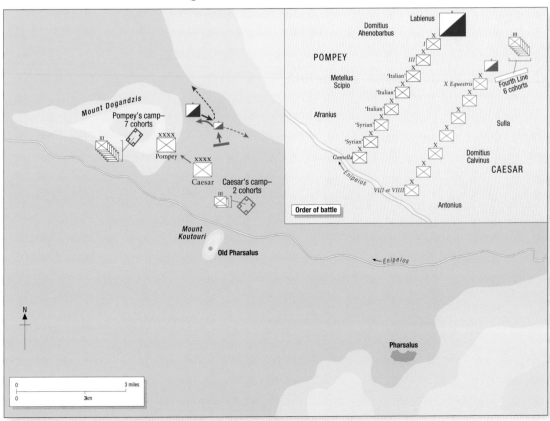

Remains of Forum Iulium (right of modern walkway), the focal point of which was the Temple of Venus Genetrix, vowed prior to Pharsalus and the most important building erected by Caesar. (Fields-Carré Collection)

The modern town of Kalambáka, with the Penios river and Píndhos range beyond. Kalambáka is the Aiginion of antiquity, 'which commands the way to Thessaly' (*BC* 3.79.9), and here Caesar joined Cnaeus Domitius Calvinus and his two veteran legions (*XI* and *XII*) before marching on Pharsalus. (Fields-Carré Collection)

the modern Fársala about 5km (3 miles) south of the river Enipeios. The site of Old Pharsalus is disputed. One possibility is that the battle was fought on the north bank of the river, at the western end of the plain, which is almost entirely closed on the remaining sides by hills. Pompey was camped on a hill at the western end of the plain, Caesar in the plain further east. Old Pharsalus was across the river, not far from the site of Caesar's camp.

Caesar's battle report, on the other hand, does allow us to see the contending armies down to the level of the individual cohorts. On paper, Pompey had the equivalent of 11 legions made up of 110 cohorts, 45,000 legionaries plus 2,000 time-expired veterans (*evocati*) at Caesar's estimation. However, this ignores the fact that Pompey had left up to 22 cohorts on detached garrison duty, so that the two sides were more evenly matched than Caesar suggests. Caesar himself was able to field eight legions in 80 under-strength cohorts, totalling 22,000 legionaries by his own reckoning (*BC* 3.88.5, 89.1).

Pompey's legions may have been stronger, but they were certainly less experienced than Caesar's. On the left were the two legions (Pompeian *I* and Caesarian *XV*) Caesar had handed over 'in obedience to the decree of the Senate at the beginning of the civil strife' (*BC* 3.88.1), now numbered *I* and *III*; in the centre were his legions from Syria, on the right *legio Gemella* from Cilicia and some cohorts that had found their way from Iberia. Lucius Domitius Ahenobarbus (*cos.* 54 BC), hot foot from the fall of Massilia, commanded the left, Quintus Caecilius Metellus Pius Scipio (*cos.* 52 BC), usually referred to as Metellus Scipio, in the centre, and the very experienced Lucius Afranius (*cos.* 60 BC) on the right. The *evocati*, who had volunteered their services, were dispersed throughout the line of battle. Having little confidence in the majority of his legionaries, Pompey ordered the cohorts to deploy ten deep and await the enemy charge at the halt, hoping to keep his raw recruits in a compact formation and prevent them from running away (Frontinus *Strategemata* 2.3.22). Pompey was relying upon his numerically superior cavalry, about 7,000 strong from at least ten nations and supported by a host of archers and slingers, to outflank Caesar's right and roll up his line.

Like Pompey's army, Caesar's was deployed in the customary *triplex acies*, but it was vital that its front should cover much the same frontage as their opponents, so his cohorts were probably formed four or even six ranks deep. Realizing the threat to his right flank, Caesar took one cohort from the third line of six of his legions and formed them into a fourth line, angled back and concealed behind his cavalry. As usual, in his order of battle, Caesar posted *legio X Equestris* on the right, and *legio VIIII* on the left, and as it had suffered heavy casualties in the Dyrrhachium engagements, he brigaded it with *legio VIII* 'so as almost to make one legion out of two, and ordered them to cooperate' (*BC* 3.89.1–2, cf. 93.8). The remaining five legions he posted in between them. Marcus Antonius was in command on the left, Cnaeus Domitius Calvinus (*cos.* 53 BC) in the centre, and Publius Cornelius Sulla, nephew of the dictator Sulla and son-in-law of Pompey, on the right. Caesar himself would spend most of the battle with *legio X Equestris*, his favourite unit, on the crucial right wing. For the battle Caesar's men were given the watchword 'Venus, Bringer of Victory' in reference to his divine ancestress, while Pompey's men put their trust in 'Hercules, Unconquered'.

Titus Atius Labienus, Caesar's former second-in-command, led Pompey's massed cavalry against the Caesarian right wing and soon put the enemy horsemen, who only numbered 1,000 or thereabouts, to flight. However, in the process these tyro-horsemen lost their order and merged into one great mass – many of the men supplied by eastern potentates were ill trained, and both Appian (*Bellum civilia* 2.76) and Plutarch (*Caesar* 45.2) describe them as young and inexperienced. Suddenly Caesar's fourth line, the back-up legionaries, burst from behind the main battle line and charged the milling throng of cavalry, stampeding them to the rear in wide-eyed flight. In the *sauve qui peut* that followed, Pompey's light-armed troops were left in the lurch and massacred or dispersed by Caesar's legionaries. Pompey's main attack had failed.

In the meantime the main infantry lines clashed, Caesar's superbly disciplined men stopping to re-form when they realized that the Pompeian cohorts were not advancing to meet them,

Faïence bowl, 16th-century Italian, decorated with scene showing the charge of Pompey's eastern cavalry against Caesar's right wing on his open flank at Pharsalus. Though gathered from ten or more nations, its numbers alone made it formidable. The cavalry plan seemed like a battle winner, worthy of Alexander himself. Yet unlike Alexander, who always fought like a Homeric hero, Pompey did not lead the charge in person. (Ancient Art & Architecture)

as was the norm, and that they had begun their charge too early. Centurions, having redressed the ranks, ordered the advance to resume. When the Caesarians were within 20m (70ft) of the enemy, they discharged their *pila* and then charged into contact with drawn swords. A fierce struggle followed, and the second-line cohorts were drawn in. In other words, the Pompeians stood their ground and vindicated their chief's battlefield tactics.

As the fourth-line cohorts swung round to threaten the now exposed left flank of the Pompeian legions and Caesar committed his third-line cohorts to add impetus to the main assault, Pompey's army collapsed. Casting aside his general's cloak, or so it was said, Pompey rode hard for the coast. For him, a dismal end to a dismal battle. His camp, in which victory banquets had been prepared and tents decked with laurel, was taken. That night Caesar dined in Pompey's tent, and 'the whole army feasted at the enemy's expense' (Appian *Bellum civilia* 2.81). When it came down to it, experience won over numbers. The Pompeians had lost the psychological advantage they would have got from making the first charge. As it was, Caesar's veterans spotted the trap. They stopped short of the Pompeian ranks to regain their breath and re-form their ranks.

Though the equipment, organization and training of the two armies were identical, it was generally agreed at the time Caesar commanded the better army. His legions, albeit battered by recent events, were made up hardened and disciplined troops from the Gallic campaigns, veterans flushed with their

Fatal crossing: Caesar on the Rubicon

On the night of 10–11 January, Caesar crossed the Rubicon into Italy accompanied by a single legion, *legio XIII*, apparently repeating, in Greek, a proverb of the time, 'let the die be cast'. So says Plutarch (*Pompey* 60.1), though usually quoted in Latin – *iacta alea est inquit*. Others suggest, as recorded by Suetonius (*DI* 32), that he quoted a line from his favourite Greek playwright Menandros, 'the die is cast', likewise usually quoted in Latin – *alea iacta est*. Either way, it is clear he had now consigned his future into the hands of the fates. The Rubicon was an otherwise insignificant muddy rivulet that separated the province of Gallia Cisalpina from Italy proper. On one side Caesar still held *imperium pro consulare* and had the right to command troops, but on the other he was a mere *privatus*, a private citizen.

We need not enter into the merits of Caesar's dispute with the Senate, suffice to say that his crossing of the Rubicon was an act of war in itself and it would thus come down to a matter of Roman soldier against Roman soldier. Caesar had reached the Rubicon in the chill of the predawn darkness and had apparently hesitated for a long time on the north bank. The consummate politician, Caesar never underestimated the momentousness of crossing the grubby watercourse into Italy. He told his men, 'we may still draw back but once across that little bridge, we shall have to fight it out' (*DI* 31.2). They crossed. For Caesar's men, after crossing the Rubicon, they had to emerge victorious. Otherwise, they would be condemned as enemies of the state and treated accordingly.

Here Caesar is on the north bank of the Rubicon. He stands alone pondering the future. A little way apart are his officers, equally pensive. In the background a group of Caesar's soldiers idly play dice by torchlight.

Left: Although badly worn, this limestone relief (Madrid, Museo Arqueológico Nacional, inv. 38418) from the Iberian fortress of Osuna, Seville, clearly shows a horseman armed with the short but deadly *falcata*, a much-favoured weapon in Iberia. (Fields-Carré Collection)

Right: Limestone relief (Madrid, Museo Arqueológico Nacional) from Osuna, Seville, depicting a warrior wearing a short woollen or linen tunic and crested (sinew?) helmet. He carries a curved, single-edged sword and a flat, oval body shield. (Fields-Carré Collection)

success and owing loyalty only to their chief. Writing about the closing stages of events in Gaul, Aulus Hirtius reports that Caesar 'had three veteran legions of exceptional valour – *VII*, *VIII* and *VIIII* – and also *XI*, a legion composed of picked men in the prime of their life, who had now seen seven years' service and of whom he had the highest hopes, although they had not yet had the same experience or reputation for mature courage as the others' (*BG* 8.8.3). On the other hand, the legions of Pompey were either inexperienced or composed of raw recruits. His more experienced formations had been irreparably lost in Iberia the previous year.

Irrespective of Pompeian deficiency in training and experience, the engagement had lasted some four hours. Caesar left his camp in the morning, then the formation for battle, then the battle, and then the pursuit. And he says his soldiers were tired, the encounter having lasted up to midday. This indicates that he considered it long. He also claims that he lost only 200 men and, because of their typically aggressive style of leadership, 'about 30 centurions, stout men' (*BC* 3.99.1). Of Pompey's army, 15,000 had died on the battlefield while 24,000 now found themselves prisoners of war. Nine eagles were captured. Most Pompeian leaders were pardoned, among them Marcus Iunius Brutus, whose mother, Servilia, had been the great love of Caesar's life, and it was even claimed that Brutus, future ringleader of Caesar's assassins, was their love child.

The battle of Thapsus

In his *Précis des Guerres de Jules César* Napoleon pulls no punches when it comes to his verdict on Caesar's Alexandrian escapade, pointing out that the Pompeians were well prepared for the campaign in Africa and a new one in Iberia. 'These two campaigns', says Napoleon, 'which demanded all his genius and good fortune to achieve victory, need never have been fought had he after Pharsalus rapidly moved against Cato and Scipio in Africa, instead of proceeding to Alexandria' (*Correspondance*, vol. XXXII, p. 63). As Cicero himself wrote in a letter to Caius Cassius Longinus, the other future ringleader of the assassins, 'the year that intervened tempted some to hope for victory, others to think lightly of defeat' (*Ad fam.* 15.15.2).

Thapsus (Ras Dimasse, Tunisia) was a port town that sat on a cape overlooking the Mediterranean, and it was here that Caesar with 20,000 legionaries, 2,000 archers and slingers and 1,200 cavalry fought a Pompeian army of 28,000 legionaries and 12,000 Gallic, Iberian and Numidian cavalry. In support were 64 Numidian elephants, split equally between the two wings, and large numbers of light-armed Numidians. Metellus Scipio and Labienus commanded the Pompeians, Iuba of Numidia the Numidians. Also present were those two Pompeian warhorses Lucius Afranius and Marcus Petreius.

Caesar had his main force of legions, which were deployed in the normal *triplex acies*, screened by light-armed troops, *legiones X Equestris* and *VIIII* forming the right of the threefold line and *legiones XIII* and *XIIII* its left. Five cohorts of *legio V Alaudae*, whose legionaries had been given a crash course in elephant fighting, were posted, along with archers and slingers, as a fourth line obliquely – as at Pharsalus – in the rear of each wing. Caesar had no intention of employing his own pachyderms in battle – he is said to have considered the lumbering, tusked bull elephant a menace to both sides. The cavalry were deployed on the right and left wings.

The battle of Thapsus, as depicted in a reproduction (dated 1619) of an original copperplate printing by the Italian architect Andrea Palladio (1508–80). Here the Caesarians are deployed for battle on the right, the Pompeians on the left with their elephants in two groups, one on each wing. The Mediterranean, however, along with the Caesarian fleet under Lucius Cispius, should be in the background, not the foreground as shown here. (Vermondo)

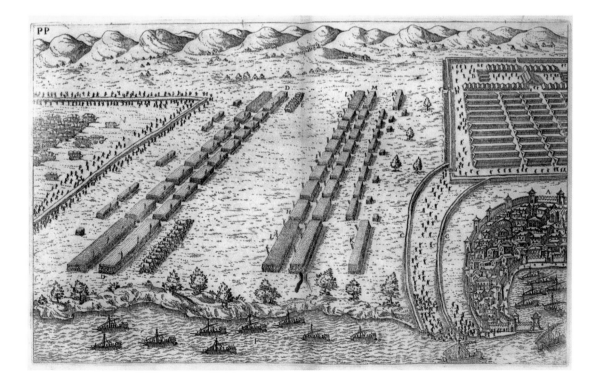

Battle of Thapsus, 6 April 46 BC

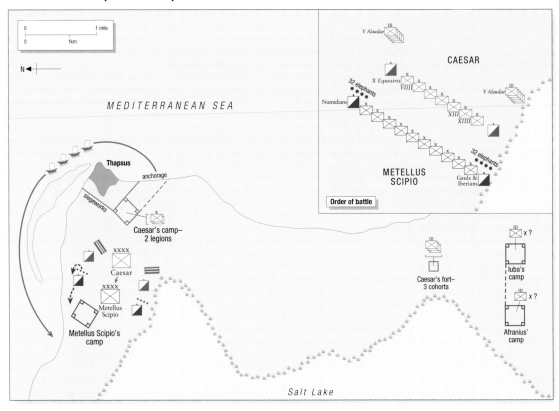

The battle began with an unauthorized charge by the Caesarians. Most of the elephants were killed, but those on the Pompeian left turned and stampeded through the troops lined up behind them (Anon. *Bellum Africum* 83.2). Caesar's famous *legio X Equestris* exploited the confusion caused, and as the Pompeian left swiftly unravelled, the rest of Metellus Scipio's line dissolved. Labienus, the irrepressible commander, escaped the carnage and reached Iberia where he joined up with Pompey's sons, Cnaeus Pompeius Magnus Minor and Sextus Pompeius Magnus Pius. Surrounded and cut down from his horse, he would die outside Munda fighting to his last breath. Likewise Afranius, Iuba and Petreius escaped, but the first was eventually captured and delivered to Caesar, who put him to death for his perfidy, and the other two, who expected no mercy from Caesar, fought a duel in which one killed the other and then killed himself. Ironically, Caesar, architect of victory, was laid low by an epileptic fit early in the battle (Plutarch *Caesar* 53.3). Even so, with this victory he had defeated the Pompeians so effectively that republican opposition in Africa ceased.

The battle of Munda

The year is 45 BC, the penultimate one for Caesar and another campaign in Iberia, where the remnants of Pompey's support had rallied round his two sons, Cnaeus and Sextus Pompeius. Caesar took *legio V Alaudae* and some of

the younger formations, including *legio III* from his consular series in 48 BC, and appears to have diverted the veterans of *VI* and *X Equestris*, who were en route to their well-earned retirements in Arelate (Arles) and Narbo (Narbonne). The only full account of the second Iberian campaign is the *Bellum Hispaniense*, by an unknown author, possibly a 'sturdy old centurion' who took part in it, and reckoned as one of the worse books in Latin literature. So be it, but we are told by our enthusiastic eyewitness that Caesar fielded eight legions and 8,000 cavalry, and Cnaeus Pompeius 13 legions, of which only four were tried and tested, and 6,000 cavalry (Anon. *Bellum Hispaniense* 30.1).

The location of this, Caesar's last and hardest-fought battle, is uncertain, but is probably near the present village of Montilla, some 32km (20 miles) south of Córdoba. When the two battle lines were about to grip, each discharged a volley of *pila*, and we are told the Pompeians 'fell in heaps'. No doubt a figure of speech and besides the advantage lay with the Pompeians because their discharge was delivered downhill. As our anonymous soldier-historian notes, 'so furious the charging with its attendant volley of missiles, that our men well nigh lost their confidence in victory' (ibid. 31.2). When battle was joined, therefore, fear seized the Caesarians, and Caesar rushed forward, removed his helmet and exhorted and shamed his men to face up to the Pompeians. As this did nothing to abate their fear, he snatched a shield from a soldier, 'said to the officers accompanying him, "This will be the end of my life and of your campaigns", and ran far out in front of line towards the enemy'. Then 'the entire army attacked at the charge and fought all day, constantly winning and losing advantage in different parts of the field, until at evening they just managed to secure victory' (Appian *Bellum civilia* 2.104).

Pursued by the victorious Caesarians, the panic-stricken Pompeians either fled to their camp or sought refuge in the fortress of Munda. In one they fought to the death, in the other they were besieged. The casualties were 1,000 Caesarians killed and 500 wounded, and of the Pompeians some 30,000 are said to have perished. Whatever the true figures, the battle would appear to have been the most stubbornly contested of the civil war. Later a veteran of the battle, on standing before Caesar in Rome, would say: 'I am not surprised that you do not recognize me. The last time we met I was whole, but at Munda my eye was gouged out, and my skull smashed in. Nor would you recognize my helmet if you could see it, for it was split by a *machaera Hispana*' (Seneca *De beneficiis* 5.24).

General view of Montilla, near Córdoba, the possible location of the battle of Munda, Caesar's final tête-à-tête with the Pompeians. When battle was joined fear seized the Caesarians, and Caesar rushed forward, removed his helmet and exhorted his men to face up to the enemy. As this did nothing to abate their fear, he snatched a shield from a soldier and sprinted towards the Pompeian line. (Paco Raya)

Genius at work

It was the military theorist Clausewitz (*Vom Krieg* 1.3) who coined the term 'military genius' to describe that combination of certain mental and intellectual attributes that enabled an individual to excel as a commander. Amongst these qualities the most important are: the cerebral ability to process large amounts of information logically and quickly and come to sound conclusions; enduring physical and moral courage; calm determination; a balanced temperament; and a sympathetic understanding of humanity. Together, these qualities produce a commander with the intangible abilities of judging the right moment – the *coup d'oeil* – and leadership. When this occurs you are left with a commander who can quickly assess the chaotic battlefield, perceive the decisive point in a battle and then lead his men through the trauma of close, violent combat to achieve the objective. Caesar was unusually well endowed with many of these qualities, but he was far from being infallible.

Napoleon, the most renowned of Caesar's self-proclaimed military successors, was said to have the ability to process large amounts of information rapidly, make a decision and then have the moral courage required to act decisively and audaciously. Caesar too had this remarkable power to act normally in the abnormal conditions of battle, and amongst his contemporaries his nervous force in a crisis was unparalleled. Seeing Pompey's dispositions on the morning of Pharsalus, Caesar made impromptu changes to his own battle line and rapidly issued orders on which units were to charge on what given signal (*BC* 3.89.2).

When we consider Caesar's *coup d'oeil*, the ability to perceive the decisive point, we need look no further than the Ilerda campaign when he steered the Pompeians almost as if they were cattle to gain an almost bloodless victory. At the very end of this operation, with his quarry well and truly corralled, Caesar was in a position to annihilate the Pompeians in battle. But he chose not to because he was quick to appreciate that 'a victory could not greatly promote his final success' (*BC* 1.82.4). Thus by refusing battle, Caesar left the two Pompeian generals, Afranius and Petreius, no option but to surrender. They sent an envoy to Caesar seeking an audience with him, 'if possible, in a place out of reach of the soldiers' (*BC* 1.84.1). He consented, but the meeting was to be held within earshot of the two armies.

The forced march to rescue Quintus Tullius Cicero, the orator's brother, from the clutches of the Nervii, or the decision not to follow Pompey across the Adriatic but to tackle the Pompeian legions in Iberia, displayed a degree of balanced temperament. A commander should endeavour to make decisions upon strategic logic, rather than an emotional basis. However, modern commentators tend to criticize Caesar for his recklessness, failing to make adequate preparations for his landings in Britannia, for instance, or invading Epeiros against much stronger opposition, but this is to misunderstand the doctrine of the Roman Army. Roman commanders habitually maintained a bold approach to their decision-making, and if they did not seek to seize the initiative and act aggressively then it was a sign that things were going very badly. The boldness of Caesar's campaigns was not markedly greater than those of many Roman commanders of the period, and certainly no different from the campaigns of Sulla or Pompey, both of whom looked for short and lively wars (Goldsworthy 1998: 76–115).

The way of the general

There is an ancient Chinese adage that runs something like this: 'A general who is stupid and brave is a calamity' (Tu Mu, commenting on Sun Tzu 8.18). As far as a general is concerned, bodily courage is but one quality and his soldiers certainly ask more of him than mere bravery. Keegan (1987: 315–38) has laid down what he sees as the five basic categories of command: first, kinship, the creation of a bond between the commander and his men; second, prescription, the direct verbal contact between the commander and his men; third, sanctions, the system of rewards and punishments operated by the commander; fourth, the imperative of action, the commander's strategic/tactical preparation and intelligence; and fifth, the imperative of example, the physical presence of the commander in battle and the sharing of risk.

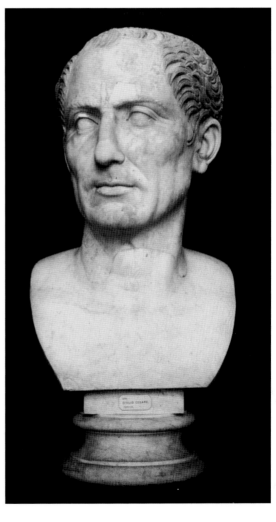

Marble bust of Caesar (Naples, Museo Archeologico Nazionale), dated to the 2nd century AD. According to Suetonius, 'Caesar is said to have been tall, fair, and well built, with a rather broad face and keen dark-brown eyes' (*DI* 45.1). He also adds that Caesar displayed a certain *amour-propre* about his hair and a fondness for wearing a laurel wreath. (Fields-Carré Collection)

Ancient battles were usually set-piece affairs in which the aim was to exhaust your opponent, and then either penetrate or outflank his line. An engagement meant a trial of strength on open ground devoid of obstacles, and so when, as was the case in a civil war, both sides were identically equipped, trained and organized – the so-called symmetry of evenly matched armies – success largely depended on superiority of numbers. Yet, as Fuller (1998: 321) reminds us, Caesar adapted the tactics of his day by basing his operations not on numerical disparity and punctilious preparations but on celerity and audacity. Put simply, speed of foot replaced numbers of men.

Of Caesar's system of warfare Suetonius says that he 'joined battle, not only after planning his movements beforehand but also on the spur of the moment, often at the end of a march, and sometimes in miserable weather, when he would be least expected to make a move' (*DI* 60.1). Appian too pinpoints the kernel, the central theme, of Caesar's concept of warfare, remarking 'he always exploited the dismay caused by his speed of execution and the fear engendered by his daring, rather than the strength created by his preparations' (*BC* 2.34). The secret of his success was in his tireless legs; victory derived from rapid marching and manoeuvring, making

Caesar's army an intricate machine of small moving parts. What is of importance in war, as Caesar fully appreciated, is extraordinary speed; velocity is victorious, and so one cannot afford to neglect an opportunity. 'When the enemy opens the outer gate', said Sun Tzu, 'one must quickly enter' (11.59 Denma Translation).

An outstanding example of this was Caesar's crossing of Mons Cevenna (Cévennes) at the end of the winter in 52 BC. The passes still had snowdrifts a couple of metres deep on them and the Arverni thought it impossible even for lone travellers to get across. But Caesar set his army to shovelling snow and was able to take the rebellious tribe totally by surprise (*BG* 7.8).

So was Caesar, with his unimaginable celerity, an outstanding military commander or not? By using Keegan's theoretical categories of command as a standard to measure by, we can make an assessment, albeit rudimentary, of Caesar's own characteristics as a commander.

First: kinship, whereby a commander should demonstrate to his men that he constantly thinks of their welfare and works for their benefit. For example,

Terminal victory: Caesar at Munda

As a commander, Caesar displayed moral courage on a regular basis. Now many men have marked physical courage, which takes no account of danger, but lack moral courage. Then again, there are men who undoubtedly possess a high moral courage, capable of great resolutions, but are very cautious about physical danger. However, Caesar was not one of these. For on the wet plain of Munda, once battle was joined, it became clear that this would be the most ferociously fought of his career. When he saw his war-trained veterans falter, he went to rally them personally, jumping from his horse and removing his helmet so they would recognize him, shaming them into standing firm. Here was a man, who only a few months before had the world at his feet, now at risk of dying on some remote southern Iberian battlefield. His men remembered seeing the look of death on his face as he plunged into the fray, and when he left the field of the slain 'he said to his friends that he had often before struggled for victory, but this was the first time that he had to fight for his life' (Plutarch *Caesar* 56.3).

The battle, in the words of Velleius Paterculus, was 'the bloodiest and most perilous Caesar had ever fought' (2.55.3). But his sudden appearance stemmed the rout, and his favourite formation, *legio X Equestris*, dug its heels in and, after a long, gruelling struggle, started to push the Pompeians back. Abandoning all pretence at discipline, the front legionaries ran for the rear. This retrograde movement was contagious and became a general scramble – a fatal attempt as it dissolved the whole battleline in a great *sauve qui peut*. As a result, the Pompeians became in a twinkling of an eye a flock of sheep. Through comprising several thousand men, *legio X Equestris* had gone into combat united as one man. For Caesar's favourites it was all in the day's work, but for Caesar himself it must have seemed as if it was his last hour. It proved the last, instead, for the Caesar's onetime lieutenant and Pompeian loyalist, Labienus.

Here the bareheaded (and frantic) Caesar pushes through the ranks among his wavering soldiers, extorting and shaming them to stand firm and fight on. Before long he will be forced to snatch a shield from one of his paralyzed soldiers.

Ponte di Tiberio, Rimini (ancient Ariminum), commissioned by Augustus (AD 14) but completed by his successor Tiberius (AD 21). Popular belief, at least in Rimini, has it that the forum of the colony of Ariminum (founded 268 BC), today's Piazza Tre Martiri, was the scene of Caesar's famous utterance *alea jacta est*. Anyway, this was the first town in Italy proper and its occupation by Caesar's *legio XIII* marked the opening of civil war. (Fototeca ENIT).

good rations and adequate billeting are of supreme importance in the exercise of command. Rations then, as now, played a very important part in a soldier's life, not just for replenishing and storing calories and energy but the undeniable fact that hot food immediately warms him up, raising not only his body temperature but morale as well. A good commander knows he has to work hard to earn the loyalty and comradeship of his men, and one way to achieve this is by ministering to their basic, workaday needs. Caesar himself appreciated that an army 'marches on its stomach', though his proper understanding of logistics was based on the assumption that the land would provide more than enough in lieu. However, as we shall see, this policy of dispensing with cumbrous convoys and allowing war to feed war could leave his men on occasions in dire straits.

Though Caesar had that rare gift of winning the hearts of those around him, and many of his soldiers would have died for him, I am not sure we can go so far to say that he actually loved the men under his command. He certainly understood that when officers were close to soldiers they were like the limbs and joints of the same body, which, in turn, meant the soldiers loved them like their kith and kin. Caesar also knew he had to bind the soldiers' affection to him, and in time a simple nod from him was better than elusive praise from another. He achieved this by making a point of close personal contact with the centurions, if not with every individual, under his command, treating them not merely as subordinates but as experienced soldiers whose advice was heeded and respected. This policy reaped it rewards.

Indeed, a crucial factor in preserving collected experience and skill in his army was the rise of the professional centurion. In a legion of Caesar's time there were 60 centurions, six in each of the ten cohorts. The highest centurial rank was that of *primus pilus*, 'first spear', the chief centurion of the legion who nominally commanded the first century in the first cohort. It was only in Caesar's day that these men become prominent. In his *commentarii*, it is the centurion more than any other grade of officer who receives attention and praise, both collectively and as named individuals. Men like Publius Sextius Baculus, *primus pilus* of the newly raised *legio XII* who was serious injured at the Sabis (*BG* 2.25.3), Marcus Cassius Scaeva who received several serious wounds and had an eye shot out with an arrow defending one of the forts at Dyrrhachium (*BC* 3.53.3–4), and Caius Crastinus who died while leading the charge at Pharsalus (*BC* 3.99.2). These men are depicted as heroic figures, men who inspire the soldiers under their command through their conspicuous courage.

During the Gallic campaigns Caesar's army more than doubled in size, creating many opportunities for promotion to higher grades of the centurionate. Thus on several occasions he notes that he promoted gallant centurions from lower grades in veteran legions to higher positions in newly raised units. Scaeva, mentioned above, was transferred from 'the eighth cohort to the post of first centurion of the first cohort' (*BC* 3.53.5), that is, *primus pilus*. An army with a high percentage of new recruits (who tired and blistered easily) does not lend itself to conquest that easily. So to beat this sloppy pudding into something solid, Caesar closely associated veterans and rookies.

Valour belongs to the rookie as well as to the veteran, but in the former it is much more evanescent. It is only by the habits of soldiering, and after several campaigns, that the soldier acquires the moral courage that allows him to bear the fatigues and privations of war without a murmur. In this way the

A 19th-century engraving showing Caesar crossing the Rubicon. The Rubicon is a stream that once formed the boundary between Roman Italy and Gallia Cisalpina, a province overseen by Caesar. By crossing it he effectively declared war on the Republic, so the phrase 'a step across the Rubicon' has come to signify an irrevocable decision that carries heavy risks. (Ancient Art & Architecture)

veterans were a valuable asset to a new legion, having gained experience in soldiering and been tempered and tested in actual combat. Thus newly raised legions were provided with a valuable cadre of experienced centurions promoted from junior grades in veteran units.

Second: prescription, whereby a commander can strengthen his position through accessibility and constant visibility. This allows the commander to exercise his personal influence on the course of the battle. Here we need look no further than Caesar's famous scarlet cloak. With his hard-pressed legionaries desperately defending the siege lines outside Alesia, Caesar knew the battle had reached its final crisis. He rode to an advantage point and began directing the battle. Finally, when the fighting became more ferocious and his men were pressed to breaking point, Caesar committed himself to the fray and the 'conspicuous colour of the cloak he habitually wore in battle proclaimed his arrival' (*BG* 7.88.1). His exhausted but inspired men raised a war-cry, threw their *pila*, and then set to work with their swords. Like Alexander they must have reckoned him invincible, and when superstitious soldiers believe a commander is blessed by the gods, it gives them complete confidence in him. So it was with Caesar, and he exploited it to the hilt.

Third: sanctions, whereby a commander must operate a just system of rewards and punishments, carefully assessing the needful balance between praise and censure to maintain the iron bonds of discipline. The best disciplinarian is he who understands his men and remembers they are human beings and treats them accordingly.

In simple approaches either the positive effects of rewards or the negative effects of punishment are employed on an individual basis, whereas more sophisticated thinkers believe in positive methods to manipulating fighting spirit and overcoming fear without the greater fear of punishment and death

The Cathedral of La Seu Vella, La Suda hill, Lérida (Catalan Lleida). This rocky eminence is the site of ancient Ilerda, the chief settlement of the Iberian Ilergetes, and its commanding position on the right bank of the Sicoris (Segre) induced the Pompeian legates, Afranius and Petreius, to make it the key of their defence against Caesar. So Ilerda was packed with five Pompeian legions and several cohorts of local levies. (Hector Blanco de Frutos)

38

as the sole motivator. Caesar himself was actuated by the imperatives of power rather than by the adjurations of moralist. So he took a cool look at the world and based his doctrine on the very imperfections of man. Self-interest was the only factor in human life sufficiently constant to base a policy on, and Caesar made use of the fact through a well-digested system of rewards and punishments. Of course, carried to its ruthless conclusion, this frank recognition of the self-interest in man became less attractive.

Caesar also believed that punishment should extend to the highest ranks and rewards to the lowest. These are the handles of leadership, the means by which to control authority and wield power. Thus soldiers who distinguished themselves were rewarded and promoted, Caesar judging them, in the words of Suetonius, 'by their fighting record, not by their morals or social position' (*DI* 65). In a similar vein Plutarch says that 'Caesar lavished generous rewards, which showed that he was not piling up wealth from his wars for his private luxury or a life of ease: rather he laid it aside in trust as a prize for bravery which was open to all' (*Caesar* 17.1). Thus the fighting spirit of his army was nurtured, and at the behest of its commander it would go through fire or water.

Having said that, Caesar did not manipulate his soldiers in combat like sheep, literally keeping them stupid. Special attention was paid to unit morale, which can be fostered through such enlightened leadership. Caesar trained his men hard, but also flattered them, fostering their pride in themselves and their unit. He created an especially close bond with *legio X Equestris*, habitually placing it on the right of his line, the position of most honour, and leading them in person. Such flattery and favours not only ensured its staunch loyalty to him, but made it one of the fiercest fighting formations of his army. When this legion, worn out by long service in foreign and civil wars, threatened to mutiny, Caesar restored order with a single, barked word, addressing them as *quirites*, civilians not soldiers. Normally commanders began addresses to their men with *milites*, soldiers. Caesar customarily began with the more flattering term *commilitones*, comrades. To him the term *commilito* was imbued with a feeling of brotherly loyalty and a sense of responsibility for the fate of his men. This inborn feeling of fraternity did not undermine Caesar's authority as leader; on the contrary, it served to enhance it. Yet now he was addressing the battle-hardened veterans as citizens, just men off the street. He was implying, of course, that he now considered them discharged from his service.

Possibly raised by Caesar personally when he was governor of Hispania Ulterior (61–60 BC), *legio X* was with him in Gaul (58–49 BC), Iberia (49 BC), and fought at Pharsalus (48 BC) and Thapsus (46 BC). The survivors were discharged en masse after 16 years service (46–45 BC), but were fighting again at Munda (45 BC). The legion's emblem was the bull, perhaps reflecting its Caesarian origin, as

Although the anonymous author of *Bellum Alexandrinum* (possibly Aulus Hirtius) barely mentions her by name (which is remarkable in itself), the thrice-married Caesar certainly succumbed to the magnetic charms of Cleopatra. No sooner had he established his lover on the throne of Egypt than he spent the next two months on a pleasure cruise with her on the Nile. (Fields-Carré Collection)

the bull was the zodiacal sign associated with Venus, legendary ancestress of the Iulii. It gained the cognomen *Equestris* after Caesar ordered some of the legion to mount up on the horses of his Gaulish cavalry and to accompany him to the parley with Ariovistus (58 BC). This prompted a wit among the soldiers to discern a further honour for this, already Caesar's favourite legion. For some time he had been treating the unit as his personal bodyguard, and now he was making all its members *equites* – the aristocratic cavalry traditionally provided by the equestrian order (*BG* 1.48.2–10). Of course, the *equites* had long since abandoned any military function and had turned into the social rank just below the senators. The actual cavalry (also *equites*) of Caesar's day consisted of auxiliaries, that is, non-Romans of inferior status to citizen legionaries. So by transferring the men of *legio X*, jokes the soldier, they are not being *de*moted but *pro*moted.

Fourth: the imperative of action, whereby the safety and security of his men should be a matter of continuing concern to the commander. In this regard, therefore, the commander himself must command an eagerness for victory. This will enable him to inspire his men with the will to win, an indomitable determination to defeat the enemy, and to endure every form of hardship and danger to achieve success. A commander animated by a truly martial spirit, Caesar involved himself in many of the details during the preparatory phase of a campaign, but once the actual operation was launched he pursued his objectives with unremitting daring, trusting to his troops and his own improvisational genius and good luck – an abstract quality that can neither be brought nor sold – to cope with any crisis. Of Alexandria Napoleon said "there seems to be nothing remarkable about the campaign… Egypt might well have become, but for Caesar's wonderful good fortune, the very grave of his reputation' (*Correspondance*, vol. XXXII, p. 63). But as Napoleon himself knew well, success in war depends more than anything else on the will to win and the good favours of fortune.

Take the calamitous winter of 54–53 BC when Caesar was faced with a major revolt of the Belgae and the Treveri precipitated by the charismatic war leader Ambiorix of the Eburones, a small but hardy tribe of what is now the Ardennes. In the flurry of events that ensued, *legio XIIII* (one of the newest formations) and five cohorts of raw recruits (perhaps the core of a new legion), under the joint command of the legates Lucius Aurunculeius Cotta and Quintus Titurius Sabinus, were surrounded and all but annihilated. The massacre of Roman troops was a huge blow to Caesar's prestige – it is noteworthy that Caesar portrays Sabinus as an inept coward – and it demonstrated to the Gauls for the first time that Caesar was vincible. As a

At the time of the Nile cruise Caesarion (Little Caesar) was conceived. Caesar moved on to other battlefields and other women, leaving the pregnant Queen of the Nile with three Roman legions (*XXVII*, *XXVIII* and *XXXVII*) to support her. Caesarion reigned as her co-ruler and heir from 44 BC until his untimely demise at the hands of Octavianus 14 years later. This is the marble bust known as the *Berlin Cleopatra* (Berlin, Altes Museum), likely of Italian provenance and made when Cleopatra was visiting Caesar in Rome. (Louis le Grand)

result, the Nervii were emboldened to mount a determined, but ultimately unsuccessful, formal siege of the winter camp held by Quintus Cicero.

With the luxury of hindsight, it is easy for us to argue that Caesar, who was relying on the supposed subjection of the Gauls, had quartered his legions unwisely far apart. With his usual luck and brilliance, however, he managed to save the situation from disaster. Yet the troops posted in their winter camps among the Belgae must have been feeling distinctly uneasy, and the recent events were a firm reminder to all and sundry that Gaul was by no means conquered. Further rebellions, even more serious, were to follow.

Fifth: the imperative of example, whereby a commander should be endowed with courage and endurance in order to establish himself in his soldiers' eyes. Personal leadership is the key to commanding soldiers, and a commander worth his salt ought to be able to do anything he asks any man in his army to do better than he can, excelling above his men in all soldierly tasks. Beyond question Caesar was a leader of this calibre, inspiring his men by his own soldierly conduct and astonishing them with 'his ability to endure physical toils that appeared to be beyond the strength of his body' (Plutarch *Caesar* 17.2).

Keegan's fifth category can be divided into three command styles: commanders who *always*, *sometimes*, or *never* enter battle. Thus at the two ends of the 'mask of command' spectrum we have the pre-state warrior chieftain of Homer exhibiting leadership in its most literal sense, and the so-called battle manager of our own age who directs as opposed to participating in combat. Here the advice given by the Hellenistic engineer Philon of Byzantium to a general besieging a city is worth consideration: 'Keep yourself out of range of missiles, or move along the lines without exposing yourself, exhort the soldiers, distribute praise and honours to those who prove their courage and berate and punish the cowards: in this way all your soldiers will confront danger as well as possible' (Philon 5.4.68–69). Philon highlights here the need for the general to raise morale by moving around and talking briefly to his men. The underlying rationale of this style of generalship is well expressed by Onasander, writing under the emperor Claudius, when he says the general 'can aid his army far less by fighting than he can harm it if he should be killed, since the knowledge of a general is far more important than his physical strength' (*Stratêgikos* 33.1). To have the greatest influence on the battle the general should stay close to, but behind his fighting line, directing and encouraging his men from this relatively safe position. Thus at Ilerda Caesar ordered up *legio VIIII* from his reserve to reinforce the fighting line, which he was himself rallying. Again, at Pharsalus Caesar

Marble bust of Iuba (Paris, musée du Louvre, Ma 1885) from Caesarea (Chercell, Algeria), dated *c.*60 BC. King of Numidia and Gaetulia since before 50 BC, he supported the Pompeian side in the civil war. After Thapsus he committed suicide, and his kingdom became a Roman province. His son would marry Cleopatra Selene, daughter of Marcus Antonius and Cleopatra. (Fields-Carré Collection)

spent most of the day just behind *legio X Equestris* on his threatened right flank. From this position he gave two signals after the advance had begun, firstly to the six cohorts in his fourth line, which only covered the right flank, and secondly, to his third line, which supported his entire main infantry line (*BC* 1.45.1, 3.93.1–94.1).

The other side

Warfare is a matter of deception. A commander worth his salt must be master of the complementary arts of simulation and dissimulation; therefore, while creating false appearances to confuse and delude the opposition, he conceals his true dispositions and ultimate intent. When capable, to echo Sun Tzu, a commander feigns incapacity; when near he makes it appear he is far away; when far away, that he is near. Deception is a means of controlling what others see and, by doing so, shaping the conclusions that they draw. The commander can shine a light on one part of the scene to focus the enemy's attention there, leaving the other parts fully imperceptible. In this way a bait or inducement might be offered the enemy by the exhibition of a weak spot to attract his eye, so the commander can fall on a key-point with superior odds. Put simply, the commander's primary target is the mind of his opposite number.

On one occasion, en route to the relief of Quintus Cicero and his legion, Caesar manipulated the size of his marching camp so as to deceive the enemy to his true strength. When encamped one night, he received intelligence that the Nervii had lifted their siege of Cicero's winter camp and were now mustering to attack him. Next morning, he broke camp at first light and marched to meet them. He had advanced only a few kilometres when he saw the Nervii on the opposite side of the valley. Caesar now takes up the story:

> It would be very risky to engage on unfavourable ground with so small a force; besides he knew that Quintus Cicero was free of the pressure of siege, so he could accept with equanimity the need to slacken the speed of his march. He halted and fortified a camp in the most advantageous position possible. The camp was already small in itself (the numbering scarcely 7,000 men, and these without baggage); even so, by making the roadways as narrow as possible he constricted it further, intending to make the enemy treat it with utter derision.
> *BG* 5.49.8–9

At dawn the following day Caesar issued orders for his cavalry to pull back within the camp and for his legionaries to heighten the ramparts on all sides and to barricade the gateways – 'and for these tasks to be carried out with much rushing about and pretence of panic as possible' (*BG* 5.50.5). In fact the barricades were sham and constructed to allow quick exit. As a result, when the overconfident Nervii drew near, the double-dealing Romans burst out of their camp with unexpected speed and put them to flight inflicting considerable loss of life.

At the core of Caesar's success was his quickness of action at both the strategic and tactical levels, the legendary *Caesariana celeritas*. For not only did Caesar always move his forces with amazing rapidity, but he also acted quickly to gain an advantage of any opportunity that presented itself. His crossing of the Rubicon with just one legion was audacious in the extreme, and Caesar's general philosophy of war, as it would be for Napoleon, was uniformly simple and to the point. Napoleon, the grandmaster of the sudden dash designed to disconcert the enemy, would later write: 'The strength of an army, like the power in mechanics, is estimated by multiplying the mass by the rapidity; a rapid march augments the morale of an army, and increases all the chances of victory' (*Maxim* IX). Steal a march to morally dominate your foe that is the nub of Napoleon's thinking here.

Yet it could be argued that Caesar was often rash and impulsive, with little or no interest in the general welfare of his army. Thus his *celeritas*, arguably his greatest trait as a commander, could sink to the level of foolhardiness and become a burden, resulting in his men being ill-supplied with basic foodstuffs. For his first visit to Britannia, and despite the season being well advanced, Caesar risked everything by leading an understrength and poorly supplied force to an unknown land across a boisterous sea. At Ilerda his men were reduced to near starvation, and at one point during the toing and froing around Dyrrhachium they had to shift as best as they could on local roots (Plutarch *Caesar* 36, 39.1). Indeed, in Africa his troopers were forced to feed seaweed to their emancipated mounts (Anon. *Bellum Africum* 24.3). Often, if his genius is shown by extracting the army from a difficult situation, sword in hand, it was his foolhardiness, which created that situation in the first place. At Gergovia and Dyrrhachium Caesar snatched a victory from a situation full of peril, much like Münchausen was able to drag himself from the swamp by means of his own hair, this turning of the tables on his enemies being executed by rapidity of movement and force of personality. Clearly Caesar's burning genius was an enigma.

A genius is a farsighted and profound individual who makes ethical evaluations beyond those of which most people are capable. Beneath the ascetic *agent provocateur* Caesar was an extremely complex individual of many contradictions. He was both bogeyman and messiah. When he was bad he was very, very bad, given to tyrannical provocation – such as when he put the elder council of the Veneti to the sword and sold the tribe into slavery, or severed the hands of the rebels at Uxellodunum. But when he was good he was great – a dynamic

Modern full-length bronze statue of Caesar, Piazza Tre Martiri, Rimini. Having taught himself in middle life how to wage war, Caesar fully understood that morale counted for more than mere numbers. Needless to say, by playing on the vanity and underlying credulity of his men, Caesar's proud and violent army gladly called to be led on to victory and glory. Hardly surprising, therefore, he later became a role model for Napoleon. (Georges Jansoone)

generator of ideas both movingly original yet glaringly obvious, the mark of a true genius. Thus his ability to lead depended much less than we suppose on his ruthlessness and readiness to practise the black arts of intimidation and suppression. His chief assets were his breath of view and self-confidence. In every emergency he was always sure he had the only workable plan.

OPPOSING COMMANDERS

During his military career, which in effect ran from his 42nd to his 55th year, Caesar faced some worthy opponents, foreign and Roman alike, men such as Ariovistus, Cassivelaunus, Afranius and Labienus. However, here we shall only look at the 'big two', namely Vercingetorix and Pompey.

Vercingetorix (d. 46 BC)

In his narrative, Caesar would have his reader believe he was bringing stability to Gaul. But Caesar's strategy of annihilation has engendered a spirit of desperation, which detonated into a revolt of Gaulish tribes under the leadership of a young prince of the Arverni, the powerful tribe who inhabited the region west of Mons Cevenna. He was called Vercingetorix, and his father Celtillus, we are told, had tried to make himself king but had been killed in internecine fighting. Setting oneself up as a king was an

Spectacular bronze sculpture of an idealized Vercingetorix, Place de Jaude, Clermont-Ferrand, by Fédéric Auguste Bartholdi (1834–1904), the Alsatian sculptor who sculpted the Statue of Liberty. It is unclear why Vercingetorix was chosen to lead the revolt, but the choice proved to be an inspired one. The young war leader was by far the most able of Caesar's opponents, giving no end of difficulties until he was trapped and besieged in Alesia. (Fabien 1309)

offence punishable by death among the more socially advanced tribes of Gaul, and by Caesar's day kingship had been abandoned in favour of elected magistrates. Vercingetorix was therefore something of social pariah who had nothing to gain from conforming, but leading a rebellion against Rome had much to offer this ambitious young dissident.

Vercingetorix had independently recruited to his cause bands of young warriors from diverse tribes – Caesar calls them 'down-and-outs and desperadoes' (*BG* 7.4.5) – and once many of the tribes supported him he quickly got to work and prepared for a showdown with Rome. He was a great speaker, who could easily win the approval of Gaulish warriors, which they customarily did by clashing their weapons. But he was also a shrewd campaigner, not prone to impetuosity like so many Gaulish chieftains, insulated as they were within their local little worlds of feuds and forays, and was to prove himself more than a match for Caesar in strategy.

Initially Vercingetorix's strategy was to draw the Romans into pitched battle, and major engagements were fought at the *oppida* of Noviodunum (?Neuvy-sur-Barangeon), Avaricum (Bourges) and Gergovia (La Roche Blanche). It was at the latter that Vercingetorix came within a hair's breadth of beating the Romans, who lost almost 700 men including 46 centurions, but Caesar just managed to pull off a pyrrhic victory. After this series of reverses, Vercingetorix realized that in pitched battle he was unable to match the Romans, who were too well trained and disciplined to be beaten in open warfare, and that it was useless to try and hold one *oppidum* after another. Therefore he decided on the one strategy that might have been successful, namely to starve the Romans by means of a 'scorched earth' policy, ensuring they would be reduced to holding only the ground upon which they encamped, procuring their supplies at the point of the sword, and having their convoys jeopardized or seized.

At a great council at Bibracte (Mount Beuvray), the largest *oppidum* of the Aedui, a popular vote unanimously confirmed Vercingetorix as the supreme commander of the joint rebel forces. He carefully explained his policy of avoiding pitched battle and wearing down the Romans by destroying all the provisions of the countryside. 'Destroy your grain and burn your granaries,' he told them, 'and this sacrifice will make you free men forever' (*BG* 7.64.5). Unfortunately, and probably understandably, the rebels could not, or would not, see that, to be effective, the work of incendiarism must be persisted in ruthlessly, and he had no means of compelling them.

His generalship in leading huge unwieldy tribal forces, both instilling fear and inspiring courage, caused Caesar great difficulties. In the event, by brilliant leadership, force of arms and occasionally sheer luck, Caesar succeeded in stamping out the revolt in a long and brutal action, which culminated in the siege of Alesia. This was to be the last significant resistance to the Roman will. It involved virtually every Gaulish tribe, including the pro-Roman Aedui, in a disastrous defeat.

Vercingetorix, without doubt, was Caesar's greatest Gallic foe, and in later times became a symbol of Gallic resistance to the threat of invasion. For the French historian and philologist Camille Jullian (1859–1933) he had the stature of a Hannibal or a Mithridates, and as a romantic national icon to the French he symbolised the heroic struggle of *la Résistance* against Hitler, the arch-imperial aggressor. On the other hand, the French essayist Michel de Montaigne (*Essais* 2.24) was not the last to question his wisdom in seeking refuge in Alesia, which thus allowed Caesar to crush the rebellion in an epic siege. Following his defeat, Vercingetorix languished for years as a prisoner in Rome, until he was garrotted after being paraded in Caesar's unprecedented quadruple triumph (Cassius Dio 49.19.4).

Pompey (106–48 BC)

The dismal end to Pompey's life should not blind us to the masterful way in which he exploited the potentialities of his situation beforehand, bursting the bonds of convention to struggle free for the next episode of his career. What is more, Pompey himself remains mute, and the absence of *commentarii* written by him means that our knowledge of him is derived from his chief antagonist, skilled both with pen and sword, the biography of the scholarly Plutarch, written long after the event, and the tart comments of the unwarlike Cicero. So his military reputation has suffered severely as a result of the damaging portrait of him penned by Caesar, who wrote, amongst other things, that Pompey 'was reluctant to let anyone stand on the same pinnacle of prestige as himself' (*BC* 1.4.6). Yet this ought not to be allowed to obscure the spectacular nature of his political ascent, much more spectacular, in fact, and much more unconstitutional than Caesar's more conventional early career. By the 60s BC Pompey was Rome's top commander, earning two extraordinary commands – clearing the Mediterranean of pirates (67 BC) and the east of Mithridates (66 BC), the first being accomplished in less than five months and the second being prolonged for some four years so he could pursue a career of eastern conquest.

The young Pompey had remained in Italy during the Cinnan regime, but discreetly retired to his ancestral lands in Picenum (Marche), on the Adriatic slopes of the Apennines, after threats were made against his life – so discreetly it was rumoured that Cinna had had him murdered. When Sulla landed at Brundisium in early 83 BC, Pompey was not slow in seeing that a vast number of aristocrats were flocking to Sulla's standard in the hope of reviving their political careers. Thus on his own initiative he raised a private army of three legions from his father's veterans and clients in Picenum and marched south to join Sulla. Hailing Pompey *imperator*, the honorific title traditionally bestowed on a victorious general by acclamation of his troops, Sulla ordered the tyro general north to clear Gallia Cisalpina of the Marians. On Sulla's victory outside the walls of Rome, his surviving opponents fled overseas, so Pompey was ordered to Sicily with six legions and a senatorial grant of extraordinary *imperium pro praetore*. Once there he quickly cleared and secured the island, executing the Marian leader, who was still legally a consul, after a show trial – earning for him the insulting nickname of *adulescentulus carnifex*, 'teenage

Colossal marble statue of Pompey (Milan, Villa Arconati a Castellazzo di Bollate) originally from Rome. The plinth bears the inscription CN(*aeus*) POMPEIVS M(*agnus*) IMP(*erator*). As for other full-length statues of Pompey, tradition has it this was the very statue that at the feet of which Caesar was assassinated. Vivid imaginations once spotted splashes of blood on the plinth. (Guido Bertolotti)

butcher' (Valerius Maximus 6.2.8). Pompey then crossed over to Africa and swiftly thrashed the leftover Marians, who had gained the support of a Numidian pretender. Pompey restored the throne to the legitimate king Hiempsal, and was hailed by his victorious troops as *imperator*. He then received instructions from Sulla ordering him to discharge all his troops save one legion, which was to stay in Africa. His army had other ideas.

Returning to Rome, with his legions still under orders, he hankered after a triumph but met with Sulla's stern opposition. Sulla pointed out that triumphs were for appointed praetors or consuls – at 24 years of age, Pompey has yet to hold a quaestorship – and, besides, triumphs for victories over Roman citizens were in bad taste. Unabashed, Pompey insisted, saying ominously 'that more people worshipped the rising than the setting sun' (Plutarch *Pompey* 14.5). Sulla could obviously have crushed Pompey if it came to a showdown, but probably felt that this was a quarrel that would bring him more trouble than profit. The ageing Sulla therefore yielded and even, though perhaps with a touch of sarcasm, confirmed the cognomen *Magnus*, 'the Great', awarded him by his army. A genius for self-promotion was to be one of the defining characteristics of Pompey's rapid and remarkable rise to power and glory.

Members of the Roman aristocracy were constantly competing among themselves for military glory and the economic rewards that accompanied it. As the stakes got higher in the late Republic, so the competition became more intense and more destructive to the political order. Pompey's career was extraordinary only in the sense that it represented, in an exaggerated form, the inherent contradictions of city-state politics played out on a Mediterranean-wide stage. Pompey was a successful soldier who undoubtedly aspired to the supremacy once held by Sulla. He was to be three times consul – on the third occasion, in 52 BC, for some months without a colleague – yet, notwithstanding his apparent power, his stiff formality stirred no exuberance and his political wavering made him generally mistrusted. Even so, we should not underestimate the man as many of his contemporaries did. By superb skill and timing he rose from his lawless beginnings as a warlord of Picenum to a constitutional pre-eminence in which he could discard the use of naked force and still pose as the defender of the Republic. As the Caesarian Sallust said of him, he was 'moderate in everything but in seeking domination' (*Historiae* 2 fr. 14 Maurenbrecher). Had Pompey won Pharsalus, the Republic could hardly have endured.

Yet compared with Caesar, Pompey was at a serious disadvantage, a superannuated man living on his past fame. Whereas Caesar had spent all but one of the last nine years at war, he had last seen active service in 62 BC, since when his prestige had sunk. Moreover, as a servant of the Senate he lacked absolute command, being as it was divided between the Pompeians and the die-hard *optimates* led by Cato, who, according to Caesar, complained that Pompey had betrayed the Republic by not making better preparations for war. So his position as generalissimo of the republican forces was undermined by senators who prodded him to actions that he might otherwise have delayed or not even have taken, and, added to this, he was saddled with two apathetic and dawdling consuls. Unity of command, Napoleon would state with absolute conviction, was 'the first necessity of war' (*Correspondance*, vol. XXXI, p. 418, note 40).

In his prime Pompey had been solid, even stolid perhaps, sensible and thorough rather than nimble-witted or inspirational. He had worked hard, trained his men hard, looked after them and gave clear orders. He gained their allegiance by proven leadership, the odd promise but never by way of high-flown phases or florid speeches. We catch a glimmer of this when Pompey addresses his soldiers in Epeiros: 'I have not abandoned, and would not abandon, the struggle on your behalf and in your company. As general and soldier, I offer myself to you' (Appian *Bellum civilia* 2.51).

A major task of an ancient general was to draw up his battle line and issue relevant orders for preplanned moves to be executed when battle was joined. Before battle Pompey could sketch out a plan that was always good, but he did not seem to have the knack to modify it according to circumstances. At Pharsalus, his one and only defeat, he had the advantage in cavalry and was so confident his 7,000 or so horsemen could carry the day that he seems to have almost held off his legionaries. As we have seen, his plan was to have all his cavalry on the left, rout their opponents and then swing in behind Caesar's legions. But Caesar, immediately seeing through Pompey's plan, took his third line of six cohorts and posted them on his right to form a fourth line, invisible to the enemy. When the cavalry attacked and routed Caesar's heavily

outnumbered horsemen, these cohorts waited until they were given the signal and then attacked so vigorously that Pompey's cavalry, startled and rattled, scattered to the four winds. After cutting down some archers and slingers, the cohorts swiftly swung in behind Pompey's main infantry line and initiated the destruction of his legions. Quality of troops was of greater value than quantity, and Caesar actually credited his victory to these six cohorts (*BC* 3.94.4). Pompey had counted on his cavalry turning and taking Caesar in the rear. Caesar parried the blow, and Pompey, seeing the failure of the means of action he counted on, was demoralized and beaten.

On the day Caesar out-gunned Pompey through a realistic appraisal of the circumstances that allowed him to take advantage of Pompey's mistakes and make instant, on-the-spot modifications; that is to say, he showed the essential value of flexibility and adaptability amidst the unpredictability of battle. Caesar clearly had a better grasp of his opponent's intentions than Pompey had of his. Had Pompey's multitude of oriental horsemen been more battle-hardened, in all probability he might have won the day. To make matters worse, they had been deployed packed too close together and after their initial success, therefore, they lost cohesion and quickly degenerated into a stationary mob. Pompey had kept no cavalry in reserve.

Pompey had placed his confidence in the material effect, Caesar in the moral effect. This is the same distinction that Napoleon drew between what he pertinently calls the terrestrial and the divine. The divine part, said he,

A 19th-century engraving depicting the assassination of Pompey as he steps on the shore of the Nile Delta. Stabbed in the back by one of his former centurions, he was then ignominiously decapitated by an Egyptian eunuch and his head taken to the boy-king, Ptolemy XIII. Meanwhile, his naked body was left unburied on the beach. And so perished Pompey the Great. (Ancient Art & Architecture)

embraces all that stems from moral forces of the character and talents, from the power to gauge your adversary and grasp the *tout ensemble*, to infuse confidence and spirit into the soldier. The terrestrial part comprises the war gear, entrenchments, orders of battle, all that consists in the mere combination or use of routine matters: it does not, of itself, gain battles.

It was here that Caesar showed his military genius, that genius which, in the ultimate analysis, Pompey lacked. Pompey's star had gone into eclipse, though we should resist any temptation to believe that he was beaten from the kick-off, so to speak. For instance, his surprise nocturnal attack by sea against an unfinished sector at the southern end of the Caesarian siege lines at Dyrrhachium showed a touch of brilliance. With mounting casualties and defeat staring him in the face, Caesar broke off the action and marched off into Greece and uncertainty. The soon-to-be-defeated Pompey was hailed *imperator* by his victorious troops (*BC* 3.71.4). It seems victory is a poor advisor.

WHEN WAR IS DONE

Tacitus, in a backward glance to earlier civil conflicts and the demolition of the republican constitution, says that Pompey was thought of as 'more inscrutable, not better [than Marius and Sulla]' (*Historiae* 2.38). When Sulla marched on Rome a generation earlier, he had been ruthless with his enemies, killing them, banishing them and seizing their property. There was a general perception the Pompeians were likely to institute a Sullan-style proscription if victorious, and many were convinced that Caesar would act the same way, particularly as he had already demonstrated in Gaul his disregard for human life. Hence the genuine surprise when Caesar instituted a policy of *clementia*, clemency, by which he deliberately sought to avoid the bloody cruelty that Sulla had shown to his defeated opponents.

Marcus Antonius delivers his funeral oration over the corpse of Caesar. Having spoken, Antonius then uncovered Caesar's body and raised his bloody toga on a spear. The Roman crowd broke loose and burned the body there and then in the Forum. (Ancient Art & Architecture)

Modern plaque bearing an excerpt from Appian's *Bellum civilia* 2.148. According to Appian, having been prevented from carrying the body up to the Capitol, the people 'brought the bier back to the Forum' and cremated the body 'on the spot where at first an altar was established, but now stands a temple that was dedicated to Caesar himself after he was deemed to merit divine honours'. (Fields-Carré Collection)

On the march to Brundisium Caesar had dashed off a letter, some time around 5 March 49 BC or thereabouts, to his political agents in Rome. In it he reveals the secret of his civil war policy: 'Let us try whether by this means we can win back the good will of all and enjoy a lasting victory, seeing that others have not managed by cruelty to escape hatred or to make their victories endure, except Lucius Sulla, whom I do not intend propose to imitate. Let this be the new style of conquest, to make mildness (*misercordia*) and generosity (*liberalitas*) our shield' (*Ad Att.* 9.7c. 1). The letter was almost certainly meant for circulation – hence the copy found amongst Cicero's correspondence – for it advertised the *clementia* for which he became famed. But this was a double-edged virtue, for forgiveness was the prerogative of kings and tyrants.

But how was Caesar going to use his victory? Suetonius, citing from a Pompeian source and not Caesar's letter, says he was not going to model himself on Sulla, a man 'who had proved himself a dunce by resigning his dictatorship' (*DI* 73). Though this remark of Caesar's was preserved by a hostile tradition keen to demonstrate his desire to overthrow the Republic, we do gain a foretaste of what Caesar was striving for from his own words as he surveyed the bloody aftermath of Pharsalus.

ARA DI CESARE

... DEPOSERO (LA SPOGLIA DI CESARE) NEL FORO, LÀ DOVE È L'ANTICA REGGIA DEI ROMANI, E VI ACCUMULARONO SOPRA TAVOLE, SEDILI E QUANTO ALTRO LEGNAME ERA LÌ. ACCESE RO IL FUOCO E TUTTO IL POPOLO ASSI STETTE AL ROGO DURANTE LA NOTTE. IN QUEL LUOGO VENNE ERETTA DAPPRIMA UN'ARA, ORA VI È IL TEMPIO DELLO STESSO CESARE, NEL QUALE EGLI È ONORATO COME UN DIO

APPIANO DI BELLO CIV II 148

Asinius Pollio records in his *Historiae* that when Caesar, at the battle of Pharsalus, saw his enemies forced to choose between massacre and flight, he said, in these words: 'They wanted it thus. They would have condemned me – me Caius Caesar – regardless of all my victories if I had not appealed to my army for help' *DI* 30.4.

It is certain that Caesar had no real intentions to restore the Republic; he wanted a system in which he was to be the big man. To achieve this, therefore, he looked around for the best and most workable example available for him to ape, namely the Hellenistic east. In a very real sense Caesar was the first emperor (full marks to the quiet and studious Suetonius), but this imperial experiment was to be cut short on the Ides of March 44 BC by men armed with no more than a glib reason as to why they had liquidated Caesar. Remove the tyrant and the Republic would revive. Hardly, for they had ignored the elemental fact that Caesar had retained his position and power through the interests of other people, interests that he had looked after. As Cicero (*Ad fam.* 9.17.2) once wrote to a friend, Caesar had bound himself to a lot of men from all sorts of backgrounds. This was one huge pressure group that had benefited from the 'Caesarian Corporation', which had been built up through a comprehensive social welfare programme, a programme that provided colonies, eradicated debt, drew up land bills, reorganized grain supplies and erected new buildings and public amenities. Under the old Republic it was a number of well-born patrons who had dispensed the grace and favours, now it was Caesar the super-patron.

When Caesar, *dictator perpetuus*, lay murdered under the statue of Pompey, symbol of the Senate's *concordia* and *libertas*, the pressure group still remained. And remain it would, seeking a Caesar substitute who would take up his mantle. Thus within days of his assassination, while the Senate dithered, the place of his funerary pyre was a shrine, and a self-appointed 'priest' was honouring him as a god. The ordinary people of Rome plainly preferred Caesar to yet more 'concord' and 'liberty' from the senatorial aristocracy.

The 'divine king'

His acceptance of the title *dictator perpetuus* demonstrates that Caesar intended to retain power indefinitely, but this then raises two further extraordinary questions. First, was Caesar seeking a quasi-divine status, and, second, was he going to convert the perpetual dictatorship into a hereditary monarchy?

This curved wall is all that remains of the Temple of Iulius Caesar and it was probably here that his corpse, along with its ivory funerary couch, was cremated by the spectators after Antonius' funeral oration. The temple itself was dedicated by Octavianus in 29 BC in honour of Divus Iulius, the 'Divine' Iulius, and to this day continues to be a site of pilgrimage. (Fields-Carré Collection)

After Thapsus the Senate, in his absence, voted Caesar a whole series of honours. The most notable of these was the statue of Caesar standing atop a globe inscribed with the legend *hemitheos*, 'demi-god'. But when Caesar returned to Rome he immediately had the inscription erased (Cassius Dio 43.14.6, 21.2). It seems that a subservient Senate was falling over itself in order to flatter Caesar and went too far in doing so on this particular occasion. With news of Munda the Senate awarded Caesar another heap of honours in his absence. Again this included an ivory statue, which was inscribed 'To the undefeated God' and carried in procession with a statue of Victory at the opening of all games in the circus. The inscription itself had strong overtones of Alexander and admittedly this is a difficult one to explain away, especially as the master of Rome did not overrule the Senate this time. Apparently his common subjects expressed a somewhat different opinion on this particular accolade. Cicero, with a touch of bitchiness, writes to his dearest friend saying the 'people are behaving splendidly in refusing to applaud Victory because of her undesirable neighbour' (*Ad Att.* 13.44.1). Still other divine honours were to follow, including a priesthood (*flamen Dialis*) established in his name as if he were a god, with Marcus Antonius appointed as his personal priest (Cicero *Philippics* 2.43.1, Cassius Dio 44.6.4). All this would culminate in the official establishment of the cult of Divus Iulius, Caesar the God, two years after his assassination.

The role of the Hellenistic king was godlike, and herein lies a possible solution to the question of Caesar's so-called divine status. It is certainly true that the divine worship of Hellenistic kings

became the model for the Roman emperors, and thus we could argue that Caesar, dictator for life, was the first example of this practice. At the public funeral of Caesar, as Suetonius says, Marcus Antonius 'instructed heralds to read, first, the recent decree simultaneously voting Caesar all divine and human honours, and then the oath by which the entire Senate had pledged themselves to watch over his safety' (*DI* 84.2). We should not forget that in his lifetime the Senate was quite prepared to grant him untold honours in order to placate their 'divine ruler'.

But why did Caesar need the more glamorous but invidious title of *rex*, especially as he now held all the power he required, ruling Rome through the position of *dictator perpetuus*?

There is the famous anecdote of the crowd hailing Caesar as *rex* when he was returning from the Latin Festival (26 January 44 BC) and he retorts with the witticism 'No, I am Caesar, not King' (*DI* 79.2). We next see Caesar, who had just accepted his position as dictator for life, presiding over the Lupercalia (15 February). Known to all readers of Shakespeare, if not of the classical sources, this was a weird and age-old ceremony in honour of Pan when young men called Luperci, wearing the skins of sacrificed goats and their foreheads smeared with the goats' blood, ran round the foot of the Palatine striking any women they met with strips of these skins so as to assist their future fertility. The Luperci were drawn from the best families of Rome, and one of their number on this particular day was Marcus Antonius. Two men, Cassius and Casca, had placed a diadem bound with laurel on Caesar's knees, but Antonius stole the moment by placing it on the recipient's head. However, Caesar blatantly refused the kingly honour, throwing the diadem into the crowd with the instruction to dedicate it to Iuppiter Capitolinus, the only king in Rome, an act that is confirmed by Cicero (*Philippics* 2.85–87), who was probably present.

It could be said that this was Caesar's way of sounding out public opinion, which proved hostile to kingship. Equally, it might have been intended to demonstrate that he did not want the title of king, or the initiative might have been entirely Antonius'. If Cassius and Casca were already up to their necks plotting Caesar's demise we can speculate that they were out to wrong foot the dictator. Unfortunately for them Antonius leaps in when he sees a golden opportunity to seek favour with Caesar. But Caesar, with lightning

Marble bust of Octavianus (Paris, musée du Louvre, Ma 1280). Four weeks after the assassination, the stripling Octavianus would style himself Caius Iulius Caesar after his adopted father. The name of Caesar would serve him well in the vicious struggles to come, and so there was certainly more than a little truth in Marcus Antonius' barrack: 'And you, boy, owe everything to your name.' (Fields-Carré Collection)

speed, steals everybody's thunder by using this moment to make a grand gesture to the populace. A clever move, as it creates an aura of negativity.

Despite the persistence of some scholars, it is highly improbable that Caesar wanted to be called *rex*, but he certainly did not want to behave in an entirely constitutional manner. Napoleon, surely a critic as qualified as any other, said: 'If Caesar wanted to be king, he would have got his army to acclaim him as such' (*Correspondance*, vol. XXXII, p. 88). Yet even though Caesar spurned the title and trappings of a king, there were many who felt he was now the king of Rome in everything but name. He was certainly the first Roman to emulate the Hellenistic kings in having his head represented on official coinage in his lifetime and had also allowed his statue to be set up in temples with those of the gods, and made of materials, namely gold and ivory, previously reserved for the gods. So whatever his future plans may have been, his present power and conduct were sufficient to bring about his untimely death. After his victory in the civil war, Caesar lived for less than a year. His dictatorship was not characterized by a proscription and confiscations of property and wealth, but there were those who wanted the Republic back, and there was no place for Caesar there.

Majolica ware, 16th-century Italian, decorated with a scene of Caesar's men destroying the bridge the migrating Helvetii had thrown over the Rhodanus (Rhône) at Genava (Geneva), an *oppidum* of the Allobroges. As Caesar only had one legion in Gallia Transalpina at the time, these men would be members of *legio X*, soon to become his *corps d'élite*. (Ancient Art & Architecture)

INSIDE THE MIND

As with many Roman military operations of the period, Caesar's invasion of Gaul was a mixture of personal self-aggrandisement, novel wealth-creation schemes for himself and his *amicitiae*, furtherance of the glory of Rome and a genuine need to keep Rome's enemies at bay. Of course Caesar would have us believe that he and his men were motivated by duty and honour, but here we must also add financial gain. Caesar himself not only paid off his astronomical debts but became extremely wealthy too, and it is certain that

many, if not most, of his officers were considerably enriched. It was well known in Rome that an appointment to Caesar's staff was a passport to wealth. The common soldiers too stood to gain, from slaves and loot. Such factors were not negligible in their support for Caesar, and he could not afford to ignore them.

One of Caesar's sternest critics was Cicero. There were many things that might have brought the two men together, such as a common appreciation for literature and mutual friends. Yet Caesar's supporters were a frightful collection of men on the make, unprincipled timeservers, the 'army of the underworld' as Cicero so gleefully described them (*Ad Att.* 9.10.7, 18.2). Unlike Cicero, who argued that the scope of war was the search for peace, Caesar looked at the problem more hardheadedly. War was meant to conquer people and establish Roman rule. The end result was to bring glory and wealth to those in the field and the citizens back home.

Above: To Caesar, and his readers, the Rhenus (Rhine) was indeed a symbolic boundary between the known and the unknown. But to say that the Rhenus was the divide between the Gauls and the Germanic tribes was little more than a convenient generalization. Leastways, Caesar was the first to bridge the river. Full-scale reconstruction (Koblenz, Festung Ehrenbreitstein) of a Roman pile driver used during the construction of Caesar's Rhine bridge in 55 BC. (Holger Weinandt)

By the end of his last year in Gaul Caesar was able return to Gallia Cisalpina content in the knowledge that his conquests and achievements would survive. For eight years Caesar and his legions had tramped up and down Gaul, each season slaughtering large numbers of people and enslaving tens of thousands of others. In many of the campaigns whole landscapes were torched. Caesar, according to Plutarch, 'had taken by storm more than 800 towns, subdued 300 nations, and of the three million men, who made up the total of those with whom at different times he fought pitched battles with, he had killed one million of them in hand-to-hand fighting and took as many more prisoners, with more than one million being sold into slavery' (*Caesar* 15.3). So some three million Gauls were lost out of a population of an estimated 12 million. Whatever their accuracy, and the population figure itself is purely conjectural, these figures reflect a perception among Caesar's contemporaries that this war against the Gauls had been something exceptional, at once terrible and splendid beyond compare. They also show Caesar's disregard for human life.

From a modern humanistic perspective, the war in Gaul, with its 'burn all, kill all, destroy all' policy, was an unjust and dirty one. Yet even Caesar's Roman biographer Suetonius did not accept his justification for the conquest

of Gaul. According to him, Caesar actually went about picking quarrels with neighbours, even allies, of Rome on the flimsiest of pretexts. Suetonius actually implies that Caesar was really after riches, and even his visits to Britannia were motivated by his greed for pearls (*DI* 24.3, 47). Similarly, Seneca condemns Caesar for his pursuit of false glory (*Epistulae* 95.37).

Glory, however, was itself a valuable commodity in Roman politics, and we ought to view his conquest of Gaul in the context of the struggle for power in what would turn out to be the closing years of the Republic. We shall, however, never know for sure why he launched his two expeditions to Britannia, nor whether he intended conquest – though there is a possible parallel in his punitive foray across the Rhenus into Germania. Caesar himself does not tell us whether he aimed at conquest or punitive action, and his only illuminating comment is that in most of his Gallic campaigns up to his first Britannic adventure he had found Britons fighting against him (*BG* 3.9.15, 4.20.2).

Whatever his true motives, and we should perhaps look no further than the simple lust for glory, Caesar's two visits made a lasting impression on the collective psyche of Rome. Britannia was a remote, almost fabled island across the *Oceanus*, a fearsome body of briny to Romans as yet unaccustomed to tidal waters outside the world of *mare nostrum*. For them Britannia lay outside the Mediterranean world around which classical civilization had flourished, 'like frogs around a frog pond' as Plato once remarked. Britannia, with its inaccessible shores, treacherous tides and wintry climate, was felt to be at the outermost edge of the world itself, a fact that lent the island an air of dangerous mystique. Gaul, Germania, Britannia, Caesar was an adventurer and showman who could not resist the lure of the next unknown. Back home the publicity was excellent as Britannia was represented as 'set apart in the unbounded Ocean', which had certainly limited the ambitions of Alexander. Even Cicero was caught up in the hype, planning to write an epic poem on the 'glorious conquest', based on front-line reports from his brother Quintus.

What was different, however, was Caesar's intellectual grasp of the nature of war. Ahead of Clausewitz, he had appreciated that war was 'a serious means to a serious end' (*Vom Krieg* 1.1.23). Caesar waged war to further his self-glorification, but each war demanded a technique of its own. In Gaul a merciless war of annihilation, whereas in Italy it was more profitable to subvert his opponent's fighting forces than exterminate them. Cruelty and clemency were but means towards gaining specific ends, and not ends in themselves.

A LIFE IN WORDS

Everyone has an opinion about Caesar, not least Caesar himself. There is a story that while 39-year-old Caesar was crossing the Alps on the way to assume his post as governor of Hispania Ulterior he came to a miserable one-horse settlement. Plutarch now takes up the narrative: 'His friends were laughing and joking about it, saying: "No doubt here too one would find people pushing themselves forward to gain office, and here too there are struggles to get the first place and jealous rivalries among the great men". Caesar then said to them in all seriousness: "As far as I am concerned I would rather be the first man here than the second in Rome"' (*Caesar* 11.2).

Much ink has been (and will be) spilt over Caesar's rise to power, and one of the great difficulties is to disentangle the true character and activities of this outstanding personality from the distortions of the legends that surround him. The Caesar as depicted by many scholars is in several important aspects very different from the self-revealed Caesar of the *commentarii* and the Caesar of the Graeco-Roman sources. Caesar's apotheosis as a superman emerged into the light of the Renaissance, and, then, soon

Cecil B. DeMille's *Cleopatra* (1934), though one of his least successful epics, did have its share of script gems, e.g. Cleopatra (Claudette Colbert): 'Together we could conquer the world'. Caesar (Warren William): 'Nice of you to include me'. William, grim, hatchet-faced, snapping brusquely over his maps and models, was a proper Caesar. (Wisconsin Center for Film and Theater Research)

became an historical obsession. We need only think of Shakespeare's Caesar, 'the foremost man of all this world?' (*Julius Caesar* II.ii.133), or Nietzsche's Caesar, 'one of those enigmatic men predestined for victory and the seduction of others' (*Beyond Good and Evil* §200).

'What drove Caius Caesar on to his own and the state's doom? Glory, ambition, and the refusal to set bounds to his own pre-eminence.' So wrote Seneca (*Epistulae* 94.65). The murder did not solve anything. The ailing Republic refused to stagger back onto its feet. Caesar had shown Rome what it was like to be ruled by one man, a kind of 'super-patron', and the huge pressure group, his 'super-clients', would not go away. As dictator for life of the Roman state he laid the foundations for sole sovereignty. Thus the sequel would be a sanguinary squabble over who was going to gain control of Caesar's legacy.

Imitation, of course, is the sincerest form of flattery. Cesare Borgia (d. 1507)

was a notorious practical imitator of his ancient Roman counterpart, albeit a far less successful one. Niccolò Machiavelli praised the achievements of both in *Il Principe*, and in the *Arte della guerra* he repeatedly turns to Caesar the general as an exemplar of military excellence. 'Thus, Julius Caesar, Alexander of Macedon, and all such men and excellent princes always fought at the head of their own armies, always marched with them on foot, and always carried their own arms; if any of them ever lost his power, he simultaneously lost his life with it and died with the same *virtù* that he had displayed while he lived' (*Arte della guerra* 7.211).

A favourite term of Machiavelli, *virtù* is a necessary quality of effective generalship and statecraft. This Machiavellian concept implies what is proper to masculine and aggressive conduct, that is to say, courage, fortitude, audacity, skill and, above all, civic spirit. The archetypal product of *virtù* is the foundation of a state or an army; the archetypal figure of *virtù* is the military hero-founder, such as Romulus. However, *virtù* may be associated with the pursuit of power and self-aggrandisement by any means and at any price. Thus Machiavelli disliked Caesar the tyrant because he destroyed the Roman Republic and its oligarchic liberties (*Discori* 1.10). Yet to the oppressed and dispirited, to the dispossessed, and to others that were under the grinding heal of poverty, Caesar became an attractive beacon. The statement of Asinius Pollio that Caesar exclaimed 'they wanted it thus'

Twentieth Century Fox's *Cleopatra* (1963) was the spectacular to end all spectaculars, with the aftermaths of Pharsalus and Philippi masterpieces of detail and Actium a top notch welter of flying projectiles and flaming wrecks. However, we may wonder if the Alexandria of Cleopatra (Elizabeth Taylor) and the Rome of Caesar (Rex Harrison) were quite as huge and shiny as the immaculate coloured scenes this extravaganza suggested. (Wisconsin Center for Film and Theater Research)

As a folk hero Caesar is immortalized in the hundreds of *camp de César* that litter the French countryside. The name was assigned indiscriminately to earthworks of all dates, but in 1861 Napoleon III sponsored an expedition, led by a distinguished soldier and scholar Colonel Stoffel (1823–1907), to discover and excavate the forts and battlefields of the Gallic campaigns. (Fields-Carré Collection)

when he viewed the Roman dead littering the field of Pharsalus sheds an enormous amount of light on Caesar's character and motives. Here was a man bigger than the system that had spawned him.

Yet the 'great man' theory of history has always been a puzzle to scholars, who search endlessly for reasons why. The real puzzle is why people actually follow these charismatic figures that mesmerize masses (and scholars) and leave rather large footprints in the sands of time. For great men to be great they need followers to make them great. Such is the case when the destiny of a nation is in the hands of a godlike individual and there is, simultaneously, a particular widespread and intense desire to return to the good old days and to innocence. This is a natural outcome of a chaotic age, and Caesar certainly made efforts to identify himself with such, which was part and parcel of the organized programme of self-glorification that made Caesar anathema to those who eventually orchestrated his removal.

Caesar was challenging the fundamentals of their world-view and we must not be distracted by the suspicion that this was a petty clash of personalities or a mere divergence of opinions. He was reckless in his single-mindedness. His recklessness might well be perceived as foolishness or arrogance, but it is a manifestation of that same strength of will which enabled him to inspire those soldiers who followed him. He was not different in kind, but manifested greater intensity of purpose than most people. Human societies, governed as they are by mediocre minds, invariably fear the turbulence of such a transforming presence, and the preservation of the current social order always necessitates some form of persecution of the catalytic figures of history, hence a sage will be mistaken for a lunatic, a saviour for a blasphemer.

BIBLIOGRAPHY

Adcock, F. E., 1956, *Caesar as a Man of Letters* Cambridge: Cambridge University Press

Balsdon, J. P. V. D., 1958, 'The Ides of March' *Historia* 7: 80–94

——, 1967, *Julius Caesar: A Political Biography* New York: Athenaeum

Beard, M., and Crawford, M.H., 1999 (2nd ed.) *Rome in the Late Republic: Problems and Interpretations* London: Duckworth

de Blois, L., 1987, *The Roman Army and Politics in the First Century before Christ* Amsterdam: J. C. Gieben

Bradford, E., 1984, *Julius Caesar: The Pursuit of Power,* London: Hamish Hamilton

Brown, R. D., 1999, 'Two Caesarian battle descriptions: a study in contrast' *Classical Journal* 94: 329-57

Brunt, P. A., 1988, *The Fall of the Roman Republic and Related Essays* Oxford: Clarendon Press

Burns, A., 1966, 'Pompey's strategy and Domitius' last stand at Corfinium' *Historia* 15: 74–95

Cawthorne, N., 2005, *Julius Caesar* London: Haus Publishing

Chrissanthos, S. G., 2001, 'Caesar and the mutiny of 47 BC' *Journal of Roman Studies* 91: 63–75

Dando-Collins, S., 2002, *Caesar's Legion: The Epic Saga of Julius Caesar's Elite Tenth Legion and the Armies of Rome* New York: John Wiley & Sons

Dodge, T. A., 1889 (repr. 2002), *The Great Captains* Stevenage: Strong Oak Press

Ezov, A., 1996, 'The "Missing Dimension" of C. Julius Caesar' *Historia* 45: 64–94

Fields, N., 2008, *The Roman Army of the Civil Wars, 90–30 BC* Oxford: Osprey (Battle Orders 34)

——, 2008, *Warlords of Republican Rome: Caesar versus Pompey* Barnsley: Pen & Sword

Fuller, J. F. C., 1965 (repr. 1998), *Julius Caesar: Man, Soldier and Tyrant* Ware: Wordsworth Editions

Gelzer, M., 1921 (trans. P. Needham 1968, repr. 1985), *Caesar: Politician and Statesman* Oxford: Blackwell

Gilliver, K., 2002, *Caesar's Gallic Wars, 58–50 BC* Oxford: Osprey (Essential Histories 43)

Goldsworthy, A. K., 1996 (repr. 1998), *The Roman Army at War, 100 BC–AD 200* Oxford: Clarendon Press

——, 2003 (repr. 2004), *In the Name of Rome: The Men who Won the Roman Empire* London: Phoenix

Grant, M., 1979, *Julius Caesar* London: Weidenfeld & Nicolson

Greenhalgh, P. A. L., 1980, *Pompey: The Roman Alexander* London: Weidenfeld & Nicolson

——, 1981, *Pompey: The Republican Prince* London: Weidenfeld & Nicolson

Gruen, E. S., 1974, *The Last Generation of the Roman Republic* Berkeley & Los Angeles: University of California Press

Harmond, J., 1969 (Diss.), *L' armée et le soldat à Rome, de 107 à 50 avant notre ère* Paris

Henderson, J., 1998, *Fighting For Rome: Poets and Caesars, History and Civil War* Cambridge: Cambridge University Press

Hillman, T. P., 1988, 'Strategic reality and the movements of Caesar, January 49 BC' *Historia* 37: 248–52

Holland, T., 2003 (repr. 2004), *Rubicon: The Triumph and Tragedy of the Roman Republic* London: Abacus

Hughes-Hallett, L., 1990, *Cleopatra: Histories, Dreams and Distortions* London: Fourth Estate

Huzar, E. G., 1978 (repr. 1986), *Mark Antony: A Biography* London: Croom Helm

Keegan, J., 1987, *The Mask of Command* London: Jonathan Cape

Keppie, L. J. F., 1984 (repr. 1998), *The Making of the Roman Army* London: Routledge

Kromayer, J., and Veith, G., 1928, *Heerwesen und Kriegführung der Griechen und Römer* München: C.H. Beck

Lacey, W. K., 1978, *Cicero and the End of the Roman Republic* London: Hodder & Stoughton

Lazenby, J. F., 1959, 'The conference at Luca and the Gallic War: a study in Roman politics, 57–55 BC' *Latomus* 18: 67–76

Leach, J., 1978 (repr. 1986), *Pompey the Great* London: Croom Helm

Le Bohec, Y., 1998, 'Vercingétorix' *Rivista storica dell' antichità* 28: 85–120

Lintott, A. W., 1968 (repr. 1999), *Violence in Republican Rome* Oxford: Clarendon Press

Meier, C., 1982 (trans. D. McLintock 1995), *Caesar* London: Harper Collins

Meyer, E., 1922 (3rd ed.), *Caesars Monarchie und das Principät des Pompejus: Innere Geschichte Roms von 66 bis 44 v. Chr.3* Stuttgart-Berlin: J.G. Cotta

Millar, F. G. B, 2002, *The Roman Republic in Political Thought* Hanover: University Press of New England

Mommsen, T., 1857, *Die Rechtsfrage zwischen Caesar und dem Senate* Breslau: M & H Marcus

Morgan, L., 1997, '*Levi quidem de re…* Julius Caesar as tyrant and pedant' *Journal of Roman Studies* 87: 23–40

Morstein-Marx, R., 2004, *Mass Oratory and Political Power in the Late Roman Republic* Cambridge: Cambridge University Press

Napoleon III, 1866, *Historie de Jules César – Tome Deuxième, Guerre des Gaules* Paris: Henri Plon

Parker, H. M. D., 1926, 'A note on the promotion of the centurions' *Journal of Roman Studies* 16: 45-52

——, 1928 (repr. 1958), *The Roman Legions* Cambridge: Heffer & Sons

Pelling, C. B. R., 1973, 'Pharsalus' *Historia* 22: 249–59

Reddé, M. (ed.), 1996, *L'armée romaine en Gaule* Paris: Éditions Errance

Rice Holmes, T., 1911 (2nd ed.), *Caesar's Conquest of Gaul* Oxford: Clarendon Press

Sabin, P., 2000, 'The face of Roman battle' *Journal of Roman Studies* 90: 1–17

Santosuosso, A., 2001 (repr. 2004), *Storming the Heavens: Soldiers, Emperors and Civilians in the Roman Empire* London: Pimlico

Seager, R. D., 2002 (2nd ed.), *Pompey the Great: A Political Biography* Oxford: Blackwell

Smith, R. D., 1958, *Service in the post-Marian Roman Army* Manchester: Manchester University Press

——, 1964, 'The significance of Caesar's consulship' *Phoenix* 18: 303–13

Stanton, G. R., 2003, 'Why did Caesar cross the Rubicon?' *Historia* 52: 67–94

Walker, S., and Highs, P., 2001, *Cleopatra of Egypt: From History to Myth* London: British Museum Press

Weinstock, S., 1971, *Divus Julius* Oxford: Oxford University Press

Welch, K., and Powell, A. (eds.), 1998, *Julius Caesar as Artful Reporter: The War Commentaries as Political Instruments* London: Duckworth

Yakobson, A., 1999, *Election and Electioneering in Rome: A Study in the Political System of the Late Republic* Stuttgart: Franz Steiner

Yavetz, Z., 1983, *Julius Caesar and his Public Image* London: Thames & Hudson

GLOSSARY

Aedile	Annually elected junior magistrate responsible for public works and games.
Amicitiae	Friends.
Cervus/cervi	Chevaux-de-frise.
Cippus/cippi	'Boundary-marker'' – sharpened stake.
Comitia centuriata	'Assembly by centuries' – popular assembly divided into five property classes, which elected consuls, praetors and military tribunes.
Cursus honorum	'Course of honours' – senatorial career structure.
Eques/equites	1. cavalryman; 2. member of equestrian order.
Evocati	Veterans recalled to the colours.
Gladius/gladii	Cut-and-thrust sword carried by legionaries.
Imperium pro consulare	Proconsular power.
Imperium pro praetore	Propraetorian power.
Lilia	'Lilies' – circular pits containing *cippi* (q.v.).
Oppidum/oppida	Fortified town.
Pilum/pila	Principal throwing weapon of legionaries.
Pontifex maximus	'Chief priest' – Rome's highest priest.
Primi ordines	'Front rankers' – six centurions of first cohort.
Proconsul	Consul whose command was prolonged.
Propraetor	Praetor whose command was prolonged.
Quaestor	Annually elected junior magistrate chiefly responsible for fiscal matters.
Scutum/scuta	Shield carried by legionaries.
Stimuli	'Stingers' – logs with iron spikes embedded in them.
Triplex acies	'Triple line-of-battle' – threefold battle line of Roman army.

INDEX

Note: figures in **bold** refer to illustrations